FACING DEATH TOGETHER
Parish Funerals

Margaret Smith, SGS

LTP

LITURGY
TRAINING
PUBLICATIONS

Distributed in Australia by Rainbow
Book Agencies/Word of Life Distributors,
303 Arthur Street, Fairfield, Vic. 3078.

ACKNOWLEDGMENTS

All scripture citations are taken from the New Revised Standard Version Bible, copyright 1989, Division of Christian Education of the National Council of Churches of Christ in the United States of America.

Excerpts from the English translation of *The Roman Missal* © 1973, International Committee on English in the Liturgy, Inc. (ICEL); excerpts from the English translation of *The Liturgy of the Hours* © 1974, ICEL; excerpts from the *Order of Christian Funerals* © 1985, ICEL. All rights reserved.

Excerpts from *Reflections on the Body, Cremation, and Catholic Funeral Rites* © 1997, United States Catholic Conference, Inc. (USCC), Washington, DC, and excerpts from Appendix to the *Order of Christian Funerals* © 1997, USCC, are used with permission. All rights reserved.

This book was designed by Joseph Conlon, typeset in Adobe Garamond by Karen Mitchell, and printed by Versa Press in East Peoria, Illinois. David Philippart was the editor, and Audrey Novak Riley was the production editor.

Art by Steve Erspamer.

Copyright © 1998, Archdiocese of Chicago: Liturgy Training Publications, 1800 North Hermitage Avenue, Chicago IL 60622-1101; 1-800-933-1800, fax 1-800-933-7094, e-mail orders@ltp.org. All rights reserved.

Library of Congress Catalog Card #98-24875

ISBN 1-56854-176-7
FUNRAL
03 02 01 00 99   5 4 3 2 1

CONTENTS

At the time of the writing of this book, the untimely and tragic death of Diana, Princess of Wales, brought the world to a standstill. The week following her death was a time of silence, waiting and collective grieving that took visible expression in rituals of placing flowers and lighting candles, often accompanied by writing expressions of sympathy, signing books of condolences or simply standing with others in silent grief. On the day of her funeral, her coffin was borne in solemn procession through the streets of London to Westminster Abbey for the inevitable formal leave-taking rites. After the service, the funeral cortege made a slow and ceremonious journey to her family's ancestral home where her body was laid to final rest.

In media coverage that flashed across the globe the world saw a planned and intentional funeral process that came to a climax in a public service of farewell, of which one publication reported: "On Saturday last week, the church channeled the nation's grief for Diana, Princess of Wales, through a unique service in Westminster Abbey."[1]

Then, at a Mass celebrated for Diana at Westminster Cathedral, Cardinal Basil Hume boldly confronted death:

Death, where is your victory? Death, where is your sting? Saint
Paul was in a defiant mood when he wrote those words . . . No,
death, you cannot defeat us. One day you will visit each one of
us, we know. Not one of us can escape from you. We recoil from you,
for we see in you an enemy, the ruthless destroyer of life, the foe
who shows no mercy. But no, death, victory will not be yours, for
we believe that Christ rose from the dead in order to open up for us
a gateway to another place where union with God locks us forever
into that endless now of ecstatic love. We were made for that. No,
death is not the end but a new beginning.[2]

On this occasion, the acutely troubling phenomenon of death
and its consequences took on a worldwide profile. Around this
death, we saw the human need to find a way and a language with
which to express the inexpressible, with which to deal with death
and the consequences it brings in its wake, and through which
a people might share its grief and proclaim the beliefs and values
it holds about death, life and the meaning of human existence.
On a world stage, a people engaged in a public and solemn ritual
process — a ritual work that somehow channeled grief, a work
that began at the place of death and concluded one week later with
a quiet laying to rest.

Confronted with death and its mysteries, Cardinal Hume
in turn confronted death with its futility and ultimate defeat.
Death raises cosmic questions about the purpose and fragility of
existence, the reality of love, the human capacity for hope in
the midst of grief, and while our Christian faith does not attempt
to solve death's mystery, it proclaims a hope in which we can
confidently taunt death with the question, "Where is your victory?"
No matter how much we recoil, one day death will visit each of us,

and will visit as friend or enemy. For people such as Francis of
Assisi, who welcomed death as "Sister," for Henri Nouwen and
Cardinal Joseph Bernardin, who could call on death to be their
friend, death was not the enemy but that gateway to another place
for which we are made. This is our Christian faith and when
death visits near us, it is the work of Christians to proclaim it.

There is no blueprint for Christian death, but Christians die
and Christians have a way of responding to death and of burying
their dead. Christians grieve and Christians have a way of hoping
in the midst of grief. Christians die and grieve, and in the face of
death and in the midst of grief Christians have a work of pastoral
and ritual care, a work of paschal faith through which they
proclaim that life, not death, has the final word.

The ritual book, the *Order of Christian Funerals* (hereafter
OCF),[3] contains within its covers a theological, pastoral and
liturgical vision that underlies the nature and purpose of this work.
This work in the face of death is one of consolation, the responsibility for which "rests with the believing community" (OCF, 9).
When death happens, the community's "principal involvement . . .
is in the celebration of the funeral rites" (OCF, 11). That celebration,
the ritual work and faith work that death demands of the
community of believers, is the main focus of this book.

The ritual work to which attention is given in these pages is
specifically that which is offered by the Catholic community. It
is important to acknowledge that we live in a multifaith and
multicultural environment. The Catholic book of rites offers a way
and a language which is not the way and language of all faith
denominations nor the way and language of all cultures. It is never
to be understood as a superior way. While this book will discuss
and reflect on the rituals of our Catholic faith as they are practiced

in predominantly Western cultures, it cannot triumphally be assumed that this way is the only way of ritualizing dying and grieving. It is simply our way.

In 1999 we end the first decade of the use of the *Order of Christian Funerals.* As this "second-generation"[4] ritual book has made its way into parish use, it has met with a variety of responses. The extent and manner of its use have varied from parish to parish, and specific issues have emerged surrounding those rituals that span the time from a person's last days through to burial and beyond. For some parishes, the *Order of Christian Funerals* may still be an unmined resource. For others, the use of the rites of this Christian funeral journey has already challenged them to ask questions about their regular Sunday worship and the connection this has with their funeral celebrations, about their ritualized ways of remembering their dead throughout the year, about the care of the bereaved throughout their journey through grief, about their baptismal responsibility to care for their dead and for those who mourn. For yet other parishes, it has been the attention that they have given to their Sunday worship that has in turn raised their consciousness of ministry at the time of death.

The purpose of this book is to help parish staffs and parish ministers to think mindfully through the intentional ritual process of the *Order of Christian Funerals,* to ponder the theological, pastoral and liturgical vision that underlies the various rituals, and to gain a sense of their potential for adaptation to particular circumstances. Readers are invited to reflect on the rites in the OCF as an environment in which a believing community can carry out its work, a work that is "rooted in that hope that comes from faith in the saving death and resurrection of the Lord Jesus Christ"

(OCF, 8), an environment to which those who mourn might bring their pain and grief.

Part I of this book takes up questions that arise around the human need for ritual expression at the time of death, the Christian response to death and the church's responsibility for the ministry of care, consolation and prayer at the time of death (Chapter 1). It explores the faith of the OCF and the unfolding of its ritual process, and thus of the community's work, from the time of death through to the time when the deceased is laid to rest (Chapter 2).

Part II invites readers to think through the specific work of each of the rites of the OCF, relating each to the timeframe around which the OCF is structured (Chapters 3, 4, 5). Discussion of each is centered on the underlying theological, pastoral and liturgical vision, the place of each in the overall ritual process and pastoral questions pertinent to each. The final chapter in this section deals with funeral rites for children (Chapter 6).

Part III attempts to deal with some of the broader questions and challenges beyond the rituals of the OCF. It discusses issues that relate to the overall liturgical and devotional life of the parish; catechesis and organization of funeral ministry as a parish moves to a new praxis; the work of the funeral director in relation to the work of the church; a ministry that makes no distinctions at the time of death; rituals at the time of removal of life support systems or mechanical ventilators (in the case of those who are brain dead); rituals for donation of organs and of the body to science.

This book is in no way intended to be a detailed commentary on the *Order of Christian Funerals,* nor is it meant to be a "how-to" manual with ready-made answers. Those who have already dared to take up the vision and challenge of the OCF will have discovered that the stance of this ritual book is a very different one than that taken in our pre–Vatican II books, which demanded a religious adherence to set rubrics. In this order, no one rite can ever be presumed to be fixed for every situation of death. Nothing is pre-packaged, and yet it is essential that a parish find its own normative but adaptable way of burying its dead and of ministering at the time of death. Far from imposing a rigidity on every funeral celebration, the rites in the OCF are intended as models for sensitive pastoral practice and for mindful adaptation to every situation of death in the parish community.

The rituals of the *Order of Christian Funerals* contain the bare bones of the celebrations of the Christian community that mark the death of a Christian. They invite those who mourn to embark on their journey through grief into Christian hope. They are bones that will remain dry and lifeless if ministers approach them without having done their own work of prayerfully reflecting on their underlying vision, or if ministers expect to find in them the final and only word. It is the task of all those who minister at the time of death to clothe these bones with living flesh. That clothing will be inspired by the life and death of the deceased, the life and grief of those who mourn, the life and story of the community that gathers and the proclamation of life founded on the death and resurrection of Jesus.

It is our hope that this book will open up new and inspirational ways of thinking about our Catholic rites surrounding dying and grieving, and inspire those who minister to use them with the attention, grace and pastoral sensitivity that is the due of our deceased and those who mourn.

CHAPTER ONE
CHRISTIANS DIE AND CHRISTIANS GRIEVE

He Could Have Been Buried as a Pauper

It was a small group of friends and acquaintances who gathered for Jim's funeral in the parish of St. Joseph — friends from the home for the elderly where he lived in a single room, friends from the senior citizens' club where he used to play cards once a week, the weekday Mass parishioners and two members of the parish pastoral care team who had visited Jim every week. Also present was Richard, a lawyer who had grown up in the parish but now lived in another area. Richard had read of Jim's death in the newspaper and remembered him from high school football days. No relatives were present — it seemed that Jim had none. It was indeed a small funeral gathering.

Jim was thought to be in his late seventies. He died leaving no papers and so no one knew his date of birth. He did have a bank account with a balance of $8.50, and it was known that he received a regular pension check. The sum total of Jim's belongings was two plastic bags containing a few pieces of clothing, his glasses and his false teeth. The president of the senior citizens' club had a photo of Jim framed and this was placed on his coffin. Jim was to be cremated and his ashes buried in the parish memorial garden. At the funeral Mass, people were invited to make a contribution toward his funeral expenses and toward a plaque that would be

placed on the memorial wall enclosing the garden. After the service,
those who had gathered for Jim's funeral were invited to the parish
house for light refreshments.

A few days after the funeral, the pastor received a letter from
Richard, congratulating the parish on the hospitality that had
been offered to Jim and to the small group who had gathered to
remember him. Jim could have been buried as a pauper.

Those who had gathered to honor Jim in his passage into fullness
of life were not the rich nor the privileged of this world — not
even biological relatives. In that very small gathering from the parish,
the church was indeed present with Jim's friends in their loss. In
a ministry of pastoral care, the church accompanied and comforted
them in their sorrow and reached out to them with the care and
consolation of Christ.

The Death of a Christian: A Church Event

This response of the parish of St. Joseph occasions reflection for
those who minister at the time of death. It poses a question: Is the
death of a Christian a private event or is it an event that concerns
and involves the church? Jim could have been one of those who
died alone and unloved, and had that been the case he would have
received the burial of a pauper — no rite to mark that he had
passed through this life, no community of faith to gather to acknowledge him as one of its own, to care for him in death and to bid
him farewell. Instead, Jim's death was a quiet summoning of the
members of the community to remember their mutual responsibility
as members of Christ's body.

The *Order of Christian Funerals* (OCF) strongly reminds the believing community of this responsibility to care for its sick and its deceased members:

> When Christians are sick, their brothers and sisters share a ministry of mutual charity . . . So too when a member of Christ's Body dies, the faithful are called to a ministry of consolation to those who have suffered the loss of one whom they love (OCF, 8).

Those who minister at the time of death do so in the context of faith grounded in the paschal mystery — the life, death and resurrection of Jesus — and at the same time bound up with membership in and identity as church. In being born into the life of Christ at baptism, the Christian is born into the life of the Christian community, a community united in and through the life, death and resurrection of Jesus. Baptism cannot be other than a communal event.

It is not surprising that if baptism is a communal event, so too is the funeral. Having first received the life of Christ in the waters of baptism, the life that unites and gives the Christian community its identity, the Christian is born into the fullness of that life in his or her own death. At the death of one of its members, the church that welcomed the new Christian in baptism gathers again to bid farewell and to hand the deceased back to God. It does so as a community united in baptismal faith.

Jim's death was a call to the baptized community of the parish of St. Joseph to remember that he had once been welcomed into the body of Christ in baptism. Through his baptism, Jim held a rightful place in the assembly of the parish of St. Joseph and so his death was a communal event for the parish community. This small gathering at St. Joseph parish recognized too, that in baptism — indeed in death — there can be no distinctions. In his suffering, poverty and anonymity Jim was deserving of the reward promised to all who bear the name of Jesus, of the hospitality of the parish and of the intercession of its members on his behalf (see OCF, 4). The circumstances of his life and death made him no less deserving than any other baptized member of the community. And so this small community of friends and caregivers came together as a ministering assembly. In this environment of care they gathered to worship God in bidding farewell to Jim and accompanying him in his final passage from this world.

The OCF does not present this ministry of the church as an option. "The responsibility for the ministry of consolation rests with the believing community" (OCF, 9). Nor is this responsibility to be divorced from the church's ministry of care for the sick. The two members of the parish pastoral care team had come to know Jim from their visits to him in the home where he lived. They had cared for him in his sickness and loneliness, and that care was not forgotten in death. "If one member suffers in the body of Christ which is the Church, all the members suffer with that member" (1 CORINTHIANS 12:26). At the time of sickness and death the members of Christ's body are called to recognize their relationship with and mutual responsibility for one another. The death of a Christian then is necessarily a church event.

The Work of Christians in the Face of Death

In the face of death and in the midst of grief, there is work to be done by the community of faith — the work of consolation and ritual. That work or ministry takes place within the context of pastoral care. There is silence in the shock and chaos of death, as the bereaved slowly begin to contemplate and adjust to death's inevitable truth. Death and its troublesome consequences summon forth the ministry of care. When grief is raw, it is easy for a pastoral minister to slip into platitudes that speak of God's will: "It must have been intended," "She is safe with God," "He is happy now," "Time will heal." But when grief is raw, such statements seem only to trivialize death. Spiritual talk about resurrection can also be out of place at this time. Jesus had to die and be buried before his disciples could experience the empty tomb. To move too quickly to talk of resurrection can often give the impression of avoiding death. The time of death and immediate grieving is the time to face death, and to go deeply into the experience of death and loss. Thus, when death happens, the work of the church is to "gently accompany the mourners in their initial adjustment to the fact of death and to the sorrow this entails" (OCF, 52). Rosa tells the story of when her father died:

> *Friends came to the house to offer their condolences. Many brought food to relieve me from cooking over these difficult days. I was appreciative of their presence and their kindness, and I know they were well-intentioned. But after a time I wanted to scream "Please, will you all go home?" They were all there with me in the house, but I realized that I needed either to be alone in my grief or, if they were going to stay, I needed them to talk about my father and to hear me as I talked about him. They were all talking about football!*

The wound of Rosa's father's death was deep. She needed the presence of people who could enter into her experience of death, who could acknowledge her grief and hear where the wound hurt most. Ministry to the bereaved calls for this kind of accompanying and gentle presence, a presence that walks with people in their grief and seeks to be where they are. It is a presence that Job's comforters had, at least in the early part of Job's trials and misery: "And they sat with him on the ground seven days and seven nights, and no one said a word to him, for they saw that his suffering was very great" (Job 2:13).

One thing that persistently leaves an impression on the family and friends of the deceased is how they were cared for, or not cared for, by the church at the time of death.

> *Paula, married to Brad, died peacefully in their home. Brad called the pastor asking that he come to anoint Paula. The pastor told him that the church no longer anointed the dead. Brad didn't know that. The pastor did not offer to come to the house to pray with Brad those prayers which at the time of death would have offered the support for which Brad was reaching out. Brad has never forgotten this unpleasant encounter.*

What a contrast to the experience of hospitality and care shown to Jim in his death, and to the small group that gathered for his funeral. Richard, who later wrote to the parish, will probably never forget that experience of pastoral care shown by the believing community of the parish of St. Joseph, of a church that took seriously its ministry of consolation at the time of death.

When a Christian dies, the church offers its consolation in a variety of ways, giving attention to the spiritual needs of the bereaved as well as to their human and psychological needs. It is not uncommon that the death of a loved one can threaten one's faith. C. S. Lewis, author and Christian thinker, wrote of this plight as he grieved his wife's untimely death. He asked how a God who is so good could allow such a thing to happen. He asked if this God in whom he passionately believed, was in fact "a spiteful imbecile who sprang a vile practical joke on even his own son on the cross".[1] With the death of his wife, Joy, Lewis's faith was thrown into disarray and he feared the loss of his belief.

Pastoral ministers can often find themselves facing this questioning. Their ministry of consolation — their work at this time — is not one of giving explanations and simplistic answers, nor indeed of preaching, but of being present with the bereaved in their sorrow and of giving quiet witness through their own faith.

At the time of death, it seems that death has the victory over life. But our baptismal faith assures us that such is not the case. It confidently asserts that in baptism the Christian joins Christ in death, and that "if in union with Christ we have imitated his death, we shall also imitate him in his resurrection" (ROMANS 6:5). The power of death is broken in Christ's death. The Australian poet Kevin Hart points us in that direction in his poem "Haranguing Death." In an eminently Christian way he soundly puts death in its place:

> Don't hide. I've had my eye on you for years
> And let me tell you straight, you're *tedious.*[2]

In full knowledge of the promise that nothing, not even death, can separate us from the love of God, the believer can well taunt death as Paul did: "Where, O death, is your victory? Where, O death, is your sting?" (1 CORINTHIANS 15:56). The work of Christians at the time of death is to offer the witness of this confident paschal faith.

As the Christian community reaches out in care and consolation, those who mourn the loss of a loved one know that in their grief they are supported by a believing community, that they can bring their grief and tears to a safe place to confront the depth of their own need of God's presence. In the midst of their loss, they know too that the faith proclaimed by this believing community lifts their focus from death to life, in the promise that human death is embraced by the death of Jesus. With the support of such faith, the bereaved know that there is an environment of care and meaning where hope and consolation are offered, where light and life are offered, not as a reward at the end of grief, but as light and life in the midst of sorrow.

CHAPTER TWO
THE FUNERAL OF A CHRISTIAN AND THE
ORDER OF CHRISTIAN FUNERALS

Death Surrounded with Ritual

In these latter years of the twentieth century our so-called civilized Western world has witnessed death through circumstances of the most horrendous kind.[1] Mass deaths in single-handed gun massacres, terrorist bombings, technological disasters, nuclear fallout, natural disasters as a result of environmental changes or imbalance — all of these have shocked nations into helplessness, bewilderment and communal reckoning. Events such as these, among many other things, have placed death and its mysteries squarely before our eyes. Yet in an age often accused of lacking a sense of ritual, our world has seen communities affected by tragic events spontaneously turn to ritualized behavior in individual and communal outpourings of grief, the sharing of pain and the search for meaning. Barely knowing what to do or say, people innately try to express the incomprehensible and the inexpressible. Bells toll, cities and workplaces come to a silent halt, politicians and churches forget differences and gather with mourners for memorial services with prayer and silence, with flickering candles, placing of flowers and litanies of lament, to mark lives cut down in death. In private and public rituals, people weep, pray, remember and communally support one another in shared grief.

One sees in these rituals of remembrance demonstrations of human needs in the face of death — the need to acknowledge death on both personal and communal levels, the need to find ways to somehow manage emotional responses to death, the need to find meaning in loss and the need to confront with other people the depths of bewilderment. At the time of death, ritual — spontaneous or structured — provides a way and a language for people to remember, and gives those who mourn a vehicle for expression of normal human emotions. Public or private rituals of words, action and silence provide necessary opportunities for people to experience and accept their grief. In public rituals, grief is brought into the company of others who share it, a company that allows dwelling unashamedly on the event of death in the midst of life, an event of mystery we dare not forget.

The structured public funeral is the ritual with which societies surround death. The funeral ritual comes about because someone has died. Obviously there is more purpose to a funeral than merely providing a means to dispose of the body. That could be done without ceremony or ritual, and without doing the many other things that people do at funerals. Funerals in our society serve many purposes. They are cultural ways for communities to care for both the deceased and for those who mourn the loss of someone they have loved. They provide religious frameworks by which communities proclaim their beliefs and values about life and death and through which people might begin to see meaning in the greatest and most troublesome mystery of life — death. They provide social frameworks in which the bereaved experience the support of the community and in which the bereaved may begin to manage their own reactions to death. They provide a ritual environment for the bereaved to begin the process of taking up new relationships in order to resume daily living. Whatever factors shape the actual form of the funeral, the funeral ritual is always intentional, meaningful and expressive.

The OCF offers a particular way of ritualizing dying and grieving. Contained in the OCF is the normative way for the Catholic community to surround death with its prayer and to proclaim its belief that "God has created each person for eternal life and that Jesus . . . by his death and resurrection, has broken the chains of sin and death that bound humanity" (OCF, 1). The OCF reminds us that "the community's principal involvement in the ministry of consolation is expressed in its active participation in the celebration of the funeral rites" (OCF, 11). Its ensemble of rites provides a rich environment of communal prayer and faith in which the assembly of believers gathers with the deceased and the bereaved to proclaim its hope in the promise that death is not the end. This proclamation is made within the deliberately ordered ritual process by which the community does its work of care and prayerful consolation.

The Perspective on Dying and Grieving in the OCF

Before beginning to think through the ritual process of the OCF, it seems important to ask how the OCF perceives dying and grieving, and what difference this makes in a context of Christian faith.

The OCF faces death directly, acknowledging the pain, suffering and consequent grief that accompany the death of a person whom one has loved. And so it must. For the crux of the Christian story and of the gospel is a death by crucifixion in which lies the seeds of life. Christians can have no stake in minimizing death. To do so is to deny that we are bearers of the image of God and that in baptism we go down into the tomb with Christ. Facing death, the church can confidently pray "for N., whom you have summoned out of this world," who has "gone from this earthly dwelling," "whose body we honor with Christian burial." In the funeral liturgy for a deceased child we have a stark confrontation with death in the words: "This body we must now bury" (OCF, 289). One of the vigil prayers, mindful of the anguish and pain of separation, asks that we find "comfort in our sadness, certainty in our doubt, and courage to live through this hour" (OCF, 80). Death is the ever-present reminder of our human condition and of the fragility of life: "The death of N. recalls our human condition and the brevity of our lives on earth." Yet for the believer, death is not the end: ". . . for those who believe in your love death is not the end, nor does it destroy the bonds that you forge in our lives" (OCF, 399).

It is significant that the pastoral notes and the models of rites offered in the OCF speak of "accompanying mourners in their initial adjustment to death" (OCF, 52), and acknowledge the potential for bewilderment, shock and heart-rending grief at the time of death. There is no voice in the OCF telling a mourner "Pull yourself together" and "Get on with life."

There is wisdom in the fact that the rites between death and the funeral liturgy focus so much on the body, for this focus challenges mourners to deal with the truth of death and the consequences of death. These rites reflect a stance that confronts death and the separation that it initiates. A body which was once alive now lies lifeless in a coffin, a harsh reminder of our mortality. The OCF offers prayer appropriate to this time of initial adjustment, prayer that can assist the grieving family and friends of the deceased as they attempt to come to grips with the unrelenting fact of death.

Alongside the necessity of adjustment to the fact of death, the OCF is sensitive to the pain of separation that is brought by death. This reality of separation is recognized throughout the OCF, although its expression is more specific in some rites than in others. Before the funeral liturgy, the rite of transfer of the body to the church or to the place of committal may be prayed. When used between the vigil and the funeral liturgy, it is a "rite of initial separation of the mourners from the deceased" (OCF, 120) who have steadfastly kept vigil with the body. This acknowledgment of separation intensifies throughout the unfolding of the ensuing rites, as the bereaved move toward a ritual moment that asks them to "acknowledge the reality of separation and commend the deceased to God" (OCF, 6). Separation becomes strikingly explicit at the time of committal, in a "rite which marks the separation in this life of the mourners from the deceased" (OCF, 213). The deliberate and intentional act of committal of the deceased, the climax of the OCF, is thus "a stark and powerful expression of this separation [which] when carried out in the midst of the community of faith . . . can help the mourners to face the end of one relationship with the deceased and to begin a new one based on prayerful remembrance, gratitude and the hope of resurrection and reunion" (OCF, 213).

In the pre–Vatican II rite of funerals there was little consciousness of or sensitivity to the fact that people were grieving. The texts and ritual actions focused almost exclusively on the deceased as sinful, and on his or her impending judgement. Even a cursory reading of some of the texts of the OCF reveals a different mindset: While the church is mindful of the deceased, the harshness of death and reality of judgment, there is a marked sensitivity to the pain and suffering of the bereaved. The OCF in fact legitimates grieving in encouraging the bereaved to bring their grief to and express it amid a supportive community of faith that shares their suffering and pain. Those planning the celebration of the rites are reminded to take into consideration "the spiritual and psychological needs of the family and friends of the deceased to express grief and their sense of loss, to accept the reality of death, and to comfort one another" (OCF, 16). The homilist is to be attentive to the grief of those present. Prayers of intercession should "truly capture the unspoken prayers and hopes of the assembly and also respond to the needs of the mourners" (OCF, 27 f).

None of the above is intended to give the impression that the OCF is an order for bereavement. The OCF is, after all, an order for funerals, and to forget this would reduce the work of our funeral rituals to that of a therapeutic tool. The ritual process of the OCF, while informed by a psychology of bereavement, is not structured around stages of grief, although it is aware that grieving and adjustment to death constitute a process to be negotiated. Its rituals contain many sources for healing, but they are not psychological tools. People do not mourn in uniform stages. At the time of any one rite, mourners are not at the same point of grief. What the OCF does acknowledge is that we have a God who is always in this mess with us, a God who carries us forward and through it and into another day. Thus, in its vision the OCF creates a ritual environment encouraging that death and its consequences be named, that grief and the pain of separation be named, expressed and heard, remembering that it is because of our faith in the promise given in the death and resurrection of Jesus that Christians can weep and pray profoundly, and remember in hope.

Dying and Grieving in the Context of Faith

Jane, attractive and personable, was the third victim of a serial murderer. She had spent the evening at a night club but did not return home. Her body was found a week later. Her family was well-known and very active in both parish and civic life. Hundreds gathered for her funeral. Just before the conclusion of the funeral liturgy, her father stood to speak, one of his close friends standing by in support. In an intense moment he spoke of the trauma of this experience of horror and obscenity. He asked the unanswerable questions: Why Jane? What kind of person could do this? Who will be the next victim? What kind of world are we living in? How can we go on? From the depths of his grief and faith he concluded with the words: "Goodbye, dear Jane. We believe that your agony is over. We cannot understand it, but we believe that you are now with God. This is the faith we have always lived by."

It is such Christian faith, faith grounded in the paschal mystery, that gives the Christian funeral its unique character. The OCF enacts and proclaims this faith in a way that transforms death from a problem to be solved to a mystery to be experienced. Confident hope in a God of compassion and recognition of loss and grief thus exist side by side in the OCF. Human death is embraced in the death of Jesus. We can confidently pray that the deceased "who has gone to rest in Christ may share in the joy of his resurrection." In the midst of death, hope is offered.

Within this context of faith, the OCF sees death as part of a movement from life to life or from baptism to baptism. "Thus we discover that our pilgrimage in faith is actually a journey from water baptism, when we are first initiated into Christ's death, to the baptism of our own death, which is the final act of incorporation into the fullness of life in Christ."[2]

A faith that can be described as life lived from baptism to baptism can proclaim with Paul that "if we have been united with him in a death like his, we will certainly be united with him in a resurrection like his" (ROMANS 6:5). As baptism is an immersion into the new life of Christ, so too the final baptism of our death is an immersion into this same — now everlasting — life.

This hope-filled faith perspective lies at the heart of the OCF. No wonder Paul can say so ardently: "But we do not want you to be uninformed, brothers and sisters, about those who have died, so that you may not grieve as others do who have no hope" (1 THESSALONIANS 4:13). In these words, Paul does not declare grieving to be inappropriate for Christians. Rather, he wants to remind Christians that we have a hope that makes it possible to face death directly and that gives permission to grieve unashamedly the loss of one whom we have loved. Precisely because of our Christian hope, Christians have the freedom to grieve more intensely. Thus, with the consolation that comes from Christian hope, the bereaved can find strength to face life without the deceased, knowing that not even death can separate us from the love of Christ.

Since the OCF sees death as part of a movement from life to life, or from baptism to baptism, there is much that is baptismal about its rites. The sacrament of baptism is an anticipation of death, ushering the new Christian into the journey that will culminate in death. Death then is celebrated in a baptismal way. The cluster of symbols by which the new Christian was welcomed in baptism — the assembly gathered around the paschal candle, the sign of the cross, the water bath, the white garment — these same symbols find a natural home in those rites with which the Christian is given farewell.

There was no way that the parish of St. Joseph would allow Jim to be buried a pauper. He was one of their own in baptism, and his death summoned them to the baptismal farewell that was his due.

The Funeral Process and the *Order of Christian Funerals*

Numerous studies on bereavement agree that it is a process to be negotiated over an indefinite period of time, and that it involves many fluctuating and often unpredictable states of thought, emotion and behavior. Death severs relational bonds that have been forged, have grown and intensified over time; death initiates a physical absence of the person whom one has loved over this time. It is not surprising that a process over time is needed if one is to accept the reality of this separation both intellectually and emotionally. Time is needed if the disarray and confusion surrounding death are to be faced in such a way as to culminate in a newly integrated state of life without the deceased.

Since the OCF is informed by a sound understanding of the dynamics of the process of bereavement, it offers a ritual process to be celebrated over a period of time. One function of such a process is to allow the time and space to "formally disentangle the deceased from the living . . . [and to] give the immediately bereaved the space and time to become used to the fact that death has occurred."[3] Psychologically, the rites give the bereaved an opportunity to begin the process of gradually untying the bonds of relationship with the deceased and formally bid farewell.

There is a sense of moving on in each of the rites of the OCF. No single rite is burdened with doing everything that must be done at the time of death. But note that what is done in ritual occurs only at the beginning of the grieving process, at a time soon after death. It touches only a limited period of time — from death to committal — within the whole experience of bereavement. Since the OCF is not an order of bereavement, the rites do not function to bring closure to grieving; expecting such would be treating them as magic. Rather, in bringing a perspective of faith to the experience of bereavement, they demonstrate a way to continue through the rest of the time of bereavement to a new state of healthy living without the deceased.

Three Ritual Moments — Not Two, Not One

The ensemble of rites in the OCF is structured around three points in time that follow a natural movement from death to committal. There is nothing new in this. These are times that the church has always observed as occasions of prayer.

THE RITUAL PROCESS OF THE OCF

Time between death and the central funeral action	◈	Vigil and Related Rites and Prayers
Time of the central funeral action	◈	Funeral Liturgy
Time after the central funeral action	◈	Rite of Committal

At work in this movement is an assumption related to the dynamics of leave-taking and bidding farewell. Psychologically, one cannot come to an acceptance of separation and leave-taking by means of a decision. One must move through this painful process at one's own pace. For some this will take longer than for others. Awareness of this dynamic contributes significantly to the way in which the OCF is structured. The church asks that the community gather with the deceased and the bereaved ideally three times — for the vigil, the funeral liturgy and the rite of committal. Each of these ritual gatherings has its own focus and work intended to support and strengthen the bereaved as the time for leave-taking and final farewell comes closer and looms larger for them.

Throughout the ritual process, the church is present in prayer and faith as it raises to memory the life of the deceased and the memory of its own story — that of Jesus, who has made the journey from death to life. At the vigil, in the time soon after death, the assembly keeps watch with the family and proclaims the saving and consoling word of God. At the funeral liturgy, the assembly, with the bereaved, gives thanks for the life of the deceased and for the life, death and resurrection of Jesus, and then commends the deceased to God. At the rite of committal, the community of faith, having accompanied the bereaved throughout the process, is present again to help the mourners in this intense and final act of leave-taking. The whole funeral process moves inevitably toward this critical moment. During the funeral process, the bereaved have known the support of the community's presence and faith. In a rich ritual environment, one that has brought the bereaved to a place before an open grave or a furnace, this potentially traumatic moment is transformed into an occasion of faith.

To attempt to do all this work in one combined rite, as today's society tempts us to do, urging us to get it all over with as quickly as possible, is both psychologically and spiritually unsound. The OCF thus offers a repertoire of rituals ordered in a process and celebrated over days of high emotional and ritual intensity. The process offers the bereaved a rich opportunity to begin to deal with the reality of death, from the time when death occurs through to the time when the deceased will be laid to rest. The focus of each of the rites is purposefully different, and each has its own appropriate time, thus enabling the bereaved to progress further in the work of separation.

Three ritual moments, not two or one, together provide a ritual framework by which the Christian community proclaims its beliefs and values in the face of the enigma of the human condition — death. The sequence of separate rites provides a rich ritual context to which the bereaved bring their grief and pain, and in which their grief is heard as they travel the painful path of separation and leave-taking. The rites offer a ritual environment in which Christian faith is brought to the mystery of death, not in an attempt to explain death away, but rather to enable believers to become more deeply steeped in the mystery of faith, grounded in a life that transforms death.

PART II
THE WORK OF OUR RITES

CHAPTER THREE

Time to Dwell with Death:
Vigil for the Deceased and Related Rites

CHAPTER FOUR

Time to Welcome, Give Thanks and
Bid Farewell: The Funeral Liturgy

CHAPTER FIVE

Time to Take Leave:
The Rite of Committal

CHAPTER SIX

Birth and Death So Close Together:
Funeral Rites for Children

CHAPTER THREE
TIME TO DWELL WITH DEATH: VIGIL FOR THE DECEASED AND RELATED RITES AND PRAYERS

The time between death and the funeral is very often one of bewilderment, shock and heart-rending grief. It is a time of silence and waiting, as those close to the deceased begin to face their grief and pain and confront the meaning of death and loss.

Kerryn tells of the time when she received the news of her brother's death while she was traveling overseas. She decided to return home for the funeral, fully aware of the long and lonely journey ahead. She recalls her relief when she took her seat on the plane and found that there were empty seats all around her. "I prayed that no one would be seated in them. I didn't want to talk. I just wanted to be alone, by myself so that I could stay in my own thoughts and memories." No one did take those seats. For Kerryn the long flight home was indeed a time of silence and waiting. It was a suspended time, an in-between time, during which Kerryn simply dwelled with death.

We become aware of the special character of this in-between time at the death of a public figure. Enveloped in a pall of silence, the body of the deceased usually lies in state in a public place, where people come to pay last respects, to mourn and to pray. The body, never left alone, lies in this place until it is to be transferred and accompanied to the place of the funeral.

For Christians, it is helpful to think of the whole time between death and the funeral as a time of waking, punctuated at certain moments with prayer — sometimes structured and public prayer that calls for the presence of the wider community of faith, and at other times more familial. The church seeks to be present with the family and friends of the deceased at this time in an "atmosphere of sensitive concern and confident faith" (OCF, 110). The OCF offers a rich and consoling body of prayer for this in-between time, to bring our Christian faith to bear on the harsh fact of death. This body of prayer takes shape in an ensemble of rites: the vigil and related rites and prayers.

These rites are "related" in that they are all opportunities for prayer during the time between death and the central funeral action. The vigil is the principal rite celebrated by the Christian community during this time. This is when the time of waking takes on a more formal and public character as the wider Christian community comes together as a liturgical assembly. By contrast, the time before the vigil is usually more private and familial, a time for informal and more intimate prayer. The related rites and prayers offer inspiration for such prayer. Since these prayers come before the vigil and other public rites, they will be discussed first.

Related Rites and Prayers

There are some moments in this time before the central funeral action that are more momentous than others: the moment of death, the time when the family first comes together, the time when the body is transferred to the funeral home to be prepared for its last journey, the time when the family and friends of the deceased first view the body, the time when the deceased is transferred to the church or the place of committal for public and formal farewell. These are the moments around which the related rites and prayers are structured.

THE RELATED RITES AND PRAYERS

Time immediately following death	◈	Prayers after Death
Time when the family first gathers to view the body	◈	Gathering in the Presence of the Body
Time when the body is transferred to the church or place of committal	◈	Transfer of the Body to the Church or Place of Committal

While these times of prayer do not require the presence of the wider community of faith, the bereaved nevertheless find the church's support and prayer in the presence of the pastoral minister. The minister, through "careful use of these rites helps the mourners to express their sorrow and to find strength and consolation through faith in Christ and his resurrection to eternal life" (OCF, 52). It can be easy for a minister to forget that these rites exist or to consider them peripheral. Yet these resources for prayer can be rich reminders of the support of the Christian community as the family begins to face its loss. Used sensitively and at opportune times, these rites "can have the effect of reassuring the mourners and of providing a consoling and helpful situation in which to pray and express their grief" (OCF, 99).

The related rites and prayers are a collection of simple, informal rites that follow a basic pattern: call to prayer, short scriptural word, response, prayer and blessing. Ritual gestures such as signing the deceased with the sign of the cross or sprinkling the deceased

with holy water find a n atural place in these intimate rites. The
published rites are intended as models of appropriate prayer
for this time; they can be freely adapted to meet a variety of circumstances and situations. They may be prayed in the home of the
deceased, the funeral home, the hospital, or some other suitable
place. These rites are not intended to be lengthy or burdensome.
They must not be overloaded with excessive words. There is a
silence in death to be respected. Prayerful silence can allow the
heart time to ponder, to pray and reflect, and simply to sit with
death. These times of prayer can be familial ritual moments,
marked by a confident paschal faith grounded in the scriptures,
moments in which the presence of the church is palpable. Families
who reach out for the church at the time of death are often at a
loss for words to pray, and the presence of the pastoral minister at
such a time can be very welcome.

Prayers after Death

The first of these rites, prayers after death, is a simple order of prayer
with scripture whose intent is to comfort the mourners in a "quiet
and prayerful response to death" (OCF, 102). It acknowledges that
death has occurred, and that in the midst of sorrow, God is present.
What a pity that Brad was denied this opportunity for comfort.
The church's prayer asks that the God of consolation:

> Be our refuge and our strength . . .
> and lift us from the depths of grief
> into the peace and light of [God's] presence (OCF, 107).

PRAYERS AFTER DEATH

❖

Invitation to prayer

Reading

The Lord's Prayer

Concluding prayer

Blessing

❖

Gathering in the Presence of the Body
The rite of gathering in the presence of the body is appropriate
when the family first gathers together around the body, as the
body is being prepared for burial, or after it has been prepared.
This is a difficult moment for mourners, for the person they knew
alive now lies lifeless before them. Death and loss are confronted
in a most immediate way. The prayer of this rite is simple and
adaptable. Short psalms of lament are at home in this rite. They
are cries of the heart that give powerful voice to grief, anguish and
helplessness. As the family gathers around the body of their loved
one, the church, in the person of the pastoral minister, is once
again present, seeking "to be with the mourners in their need and
to provide an atmosphere of sensitive concern and confident faith"
(OCF, 110).

GATHERING IN THE PRESENCE OF THE BODY

◈

Sign of the cross

Scripture verse

Sprinkling with holy water

Psalm

The Lord's Prayer

Concluding prayer

Blessing

◈

The Transfer of the Body to the Church or Place of Committal
The potential of the rite of transfer of the body to the church or
to the place of committal is yet to be realized. It is envisioned
as "a rite of initial separation of the mourners from the deceased"
(OCF, 120). This moment is an occasion of great emotion for
the mourners, as the proximity of final farewell is brought to the
surface. The place and character of this rite are evident in the
funerals of public figures when, after lying in state, the body, usually
accompanied by chief mourners, is taken in formal procession to
the place where it is to be publicly bid farewell. In the OCF, this
rite of transfer is an intimate rite, intended to be prayed "with the
family and close friends as they prepare to accompany the body
of the deceased to the church or to the place of committal"
(OCF, 119). It is a transitional and processional rite.

After the concluding prayer of this short rite, there is an instruction: "The minister invites those present to pray in silence while all is made ready for the procession" (OCF, 125). The rite is not specific about the nature of this readiness. However, this might be an opportunity for those present to approach the deceased and offer some gesture of farewell. It might also be the time for personal effects to be removed or placed in the coffin, if desired. Certainly this would be the time for a ritual closing of the coffin. With the closing, the body is ready for its pilgrimage to the church or the place of committal. The closing of the coffin may be done in silence; the action is powerful in itself. The Irish rite provides a poignant text that may be prayed before, during or after the closing:

> May God enfold you in his love
> and bring you to eternal life.
> We will pray for you, N.,
> may you pray for us.
> May God and Mary be with you.[1]

The intention of the ritual closing is that the coffin not be re-opened, for the closing is a further step in the process of leave-taking. With the funeral liturgy, it signifies the time to move on, time for public farewell. To re-open the coffin at the church for the benefit of mourners who were unable to view the body previously interrupts the ritual experience. It would be better for all mourners to pray the rite of transfer of the body at the funeral home. If this is not possible, then perhaps a private viewing could be arranged at the church well before the funeral liturgy followed by a private farewell by the family and ritual closing of the coffin. In such a situation, the rite needs to be scheduled at the time of the arrival of the body at the church before the funeral liturgy. Meanwhile the wider community of family, friends and the parish are also at the church, waiting to receive the deceased into their midst for the last time.

If the funeral liturgy does not take place at church, but at the place where the body has been waked, then the rite of transfer is used after the funeral and before transferring the body to the place of committal.

At this point in the implementation of the OCF, this rite is rarely used, but there is no reason why, in time, it would not become standard practice. If the rite of transfer is to be used in the way it is intended there is need for catechesis. Catholic funeral directors can be encouraged to use this rite instead of simply reciting a few Our Fathers and Hail Marys. How appropriate that the family be with the body as it is transferred to the place where it will be publicly bid farewell and to surround this moment with prayer.

The words that conclude this rite of initial leave-taking poignantly invite those present to join in the procession to the church or place of committal:

> The Lord guards our coming in and our going out.
> May God be with us today
> as we make this last journey with N. (OCF, 126).

TRANSFER OF THE BODY TO THE CHURCH OR TO THE PLACE OF COMMITTAL

◈

Invitation

Scripture verse

Litany

The Lord's Prayer

Concluding prayer

Invitation to the procession

Procession to the church or
to the place of committal

◈

Who Knows about These Prayers? Who Can Lead Them?
Who knows about these rites and prayers? How does the wider
community come to know about them? Who can lead them?
Brad's experience is probably not an isolated case, even now when
we are more sensitive to ritual. It is understandable that he asked
the priest to anoint the body of his wife, since that is what he had
known and no one had told him of another way. It is natural
to ask for what we know until we know there are alternatives and
know the reasons for those alternatives. Hence, it is imperative
that pastoral ministers appreciate the possibilities for prayer during
this time before the funeral liturgy, and that they sensitively offer

the presence of the church at these key moments during the time of waking.

Perhaps the related rites and prayers presume that the bereaved family already has a tradition of household prayer. We may presume that if a family does not have such a tradition, people will be uneasy about praying together. This is all the more reason for the minister to be present on the occasion of death, offering this rite. The people of God are often unwittingly left in ignorance of the richness of the church's prayer. Households of whatever nature do not normally have access to the church's ritual books. But no household will remain untouched by sickness and death. The models of prayer offered in the related rites and prayers are domestic by nature and should not be kept in locked sacristy cupboards. It is helpful and important that pastoral ministers make these household prayers from the *Order of Christian Funerals* and the *Pastoral Care of the Sick* available to the whole community in easily used and attractive booklets.[2] Thus we help each other find ready words and ritual actions to give voice to prayer.

The related rites and prayers do not necessarily call for the presence of a priest to lead the prayer. The occasion of death calls for the presence of the *church.* In the ministry of consolation and witness of faith, any member of the Christian community may lead prayer. No matter what the circumstances of death, no household or member of the community should be deprived of the presence of the church because a priest is not available. The related rites and prayers may be led by all who minister to the bereaved in this difficult time. If the church is to offer its ministry of care at the times of both sickness and death, there is need, particularly in larger parishes, for an organized ministry through which the bereaved may know the support of the community's prayer. The organization of such a ministry calls for the formation of its members in both the nature of their ministry and in the spirit of the OCF.

The Vigil for the Deceased: The Best-Kept Secret

Sister Helen was much loved in the parish, and when she died, her funeral was truly a parish occasion. The vigil celebration for Helen took place in the parish church, and because of that it began with the rite of reception. Helen was welcomed by the community in the baptismal way that this rite calls for — with candle, water, cross, white pall. As the pallbearers (Helen's nephews) carried the coffin into the church, the assembly sang a quiet processional song that voiced their grief and their faith. At this point in the vigil, one of the men in the assembly leaned over to a sister in Helen's community and asked: "Is this kind of thing only for nuns?"

These rites are for the church — the whole church. It is the right of all the baptized to have access to them, and the duty of parish pastors and other ministers to provide them. Unfortunately, one of the best-kept secrets of the OCF is the vigil for the deceased.

At a certain point in the time of waking, the church encourages the nocturnal celebration of the vigil for the deceased, the "principal rite celebrated by the Christian community in the time following death and before the funeral liturgy" (OCF, 54). The experience of some form of prayer on the eve of the funeral has always been part of Catholic practice. The community of faith has often practiced it in the rosary, during which it contemplates the life, death and resurrection of Jesus. The revised OCF has reclaimed the liturgical character of this night-watch gathering of faith, grounding the prayer in the proclamation of, and response to, the word of God.

With the vigil, the time of waking takes on a more formal and public character as the wider Christian community comes together as a liturgical assembly "to keep watch with the family in prayer . . . and find strength in Christ's presence" (OCF, 55). This is when the parish offers its first communal act of worship to God and act of consolation to the bereaved, in its supportive presence and its turning "to God's word as the source of faith and hope, as light and life in the face of . . . death" (OCF, 56). This first of the major ritual moments in the funeral process is a night hour of keeping watch, an opportunity for the bereaved to rest in death with a word that consoles and that inspires faith. To this watchful and praying assembly of believers the bereaved bring their memories of the deceased, their grief and their loss, and in that context begin their formal leave-taking.

The solemn proclamation of the word of God is at the heart of any vigil, and so too at the heart of the vigil for the deceased. We have excellent models in the Easter and Pentecost vigils, during which we keep prayerful watch with the word of God as our inspiration. The vigil for the deceased is intended to be a meeting-place of words and stories, a place for God's word to embrace the words of grief and memories of the bereaved. Deeply conscious of loss, the church proclaims its word of hope and consolation which "tells of God's design for a world in which suffering and death will relinquish their hold on all whom God has called his own" (OCF, 56). In the proclamation of the word of God, the human story of dying meets another story of dying that catches up death and transforms it into life.

It is not surprising that the OCF offers a liturgy of the word as the principal model of prayer for this vigil, the proclamation of the word being the "high point and central focus" (OCF, 59). Most people are familiar with this ritual order from their experiences of Mass. The purpose of the readings is to inspire faith and offer the consolation of a God who is always compassionate and merciful. Pastoral ministers need to be familiar with the selection of readings offered in the OCF and at the same time free to suggest readings from other parts of the scriptures. Some diocesan worship offices have published the readings from the OCF (often with the prayers) in attractive small books.[3] These can be useful tools in helping families to mull over the scriptures and to select appropriate readings.

In preparing the vigil service, the choice of readings will be determined predominantly by the life of the deceased and the needs of the bereaved. This always requires sensitivity and care. Whatever the circumstances of death or the state of the faith of the deceased and the bereaved, the assembly's work is to announce the good news that God is compassionate and that suffering and death are not the last word. Having heard this word proclaimed in its midst, the community can turn to God in confident prayer for the deceased, for all who mourn and for itself.

The pastoral notes are clear that the word of God is the abiding source of faith and hope in this time of loss. At the same time, ministers are reminded that part of their work is also to "gently accompany the mourners in their initial adjustment to the fact of death and to the sorrow this entails [and to help] the mourners to express their sorrow" (OCF, 52). The time between death and the funeral, when ordinary life is suspended, is often filled with story-telling, which is integral to the negotiation of grief. This story-telling can find a natural home in the vigil as part of the assembly's action.

As with any liturgy of the word, singing is an integral part of the vigil for the deceased. The rite calls explicitly for an opening song. At the very least, the responsorial psalm must be sung. Perhaps this is the psalm that will also be sung at the funeral liturgy. It could be a setting used at other times of the liturgical year, one that the parish knows well. If there is no one to sing the verses, all can sing the refrain with a reader proclaiming the verses. The Our Father can be chanted easily by every assembly.

The vigil encourages the retelling of the story of the deceased in multiple ways — in its symbolic actions, prayers, the scriptural word, the songs, as well as in a specific invitation to a family member or friend to speak in remembrance of the deceased. Although the rite does not say so, this invitation can surely be extended to colleagues, neighbors and others in the assembly. These words of remembrance work particularly well in informal settings. In such settings, it is important that the pastoral minister be particularly attuned to the mood and dynamic of the gathering, so that he or she can sense the opportune time for the proclamation of God's word.

In whatever setting the vigil is celebrated, the intent of the OCF is that God's word be solemnly proclaimed and heard — not merely rattled off. Silence is therefore necessary, with periods of silence suited to the assembly. Thus it is, in the context of a word that brings hope, family and friends can freely tell their stories, knowing that because they have a hope, they can enter into the story of the deceased and their own grief more deeply and intensely. Therein lies one of the greatest challenges of the vigil for the deceased.

The OCF states that the vigil may be celebrated in the church, in the home of the deceased, in the funeral home, parlor or chapel of rest, or in some other suitable place. It does not specify the presence of the body (although it may presume it), but it certainly seems that wherever possible the body ought to be the central symbol in this vigil prayer, and that the vigil ought to be celebrated wherever the body is.

Since the vigil is the first of the public ritual moments in the funeral process—when the Christian community gathers to console the bereaved—then perhaps the church is the most fitting place for the celebration. If so, the OCF suggests that the celebration begin with the rite of reception of the body.[4] Some newer church buildings have a vigil chapel so that when the body rests in the church overnight, other parish functions do not detract from the vigil. However, in some places it may not be possible for the body to rest in the church overnight, due to local laws governing where the body is kept and who is legally responsible for its safekeeping. Pastoral ministers will be guided by the flexibility that the OCF allows and by sensitivity to pastoral needs.

The practice in both the United States and Canada seems to be that the vigil is celebrated, more often than not, in the funeral home. The OCF allows for this possibility, but the ministry of pastoral care and prayer must remain where it rightly belongs— with the community of faith. "The community's principal involvement in the ministry of consolation is expressed in its active participation in the celebration of the funeral rites, particularly the vigil for the deceased, the funeral liturgy, and the rite of committal" (OCF, 11). If the parish church is particularly large and there is no chapel, a more intimate room in the funeral home might very well be the best place for this nocturnal celebration. In such cases pastoral ministers will work to ensure the essential liturgical nature of this gathering, a true occasion of keeping watch with the family in prayer, and of keeping watch with the word of God as the community's source of hope.

This ministry belongs to the believing community and not to the funeral industry. The practice of celebrating the vigil for the deceased at the funeral home is to be questioned if this comes about because of the tendency for the funeral industry to take on more and more of the care which rightly belongs to the family or to the parish. Wherever the vigil is celebrated, it is the church's responsibility and right to minister in prayer. This includes determining the best arrangement of seats, the use of real candles and perhaps incense, during intercessions, for example, and a place for proclaiming the word of God more fitting than a lecture-room style lectern. Parishes that work consistently with certain funeral homes should provide appropriate items for the vigil.

VIGIL FOR THE DECEASED
[WITH RITE OF RECEPTION]

Introductory rites

Greeting

[Sprinkling with holy water]

[Placing of the pall]

[Entrance procession]

Opening song

[Placing of Christian symbols]

Invitation to prayer

Opening prayer

Liturgy of the word

First reading and silence

Responsorial psalm

Gospel

Homily

Prayer of intercession

Litany

The Lord's Prayer

Concluding prayer

Concluding rite

Blessing

❖

Pastoral Considerations around the Vigil for the Deceased

Use of Personal Mementos in the Vigil for the Deceased. In the days immediately following death, ordinary life is put on hold, and the bereaved often find themselves in an almost timeless space as they cherish the memory of the deceased, reliving last days and treasured times with the deceased, recounting again and again the events surrounding the death of the loved one. This remembering at this time and in the months beyond these days of emotional intensity is a natural part of grieving. It is ultimately a crucial factor in being able to live in hope.

This remembering is often connected with personal mementos associated with the deceased, and the bereaved frequently request that these have some place in the funeral rites. The OCF does not address this issue except in the case of a vigil for a deceased child. Here it says:

> If, for example, a large number of children are present or if the vigil is held in the home of the deceased child, elements of the rite may be simplified or shortened and other elements or symbols that have special meaning for those taking part may be incorporated into the celebration. (OCF, 246)

Except for that statement, the OCF has nothing to say about the incorporation of personal mementos at the vigil. It is, however, quite specific when it comes to the funeral liturgy. This issue will be taken up in the following chapter.

The practice of incorporating personal mementos into our funeral gatherings is a fairly recent phenomenon. It is important that pastoral ministers be attentive to what might be behind it. Perhaps it is rooted in the past, when the Catholic funeral was often somber, with a strong emphasis on the sinfulness of the deceased and the need for forgiveness. There is a valid and healthy sense within the Christian community today that funerals be personal and human, and that there need to be room in them for multi-faceted remembrance of the deceased and for expression of grief in ways other than words. The value of mementos is that, if used sensitively, they are another source of consolation and support for the family and friends. Their use can elicit other memories and conversation, thus serving as occasions for thanksgiving or lament.

A sensitive and attuned pastoral minister can sense the ripe moments for such thanksgiving and lament.

The challenge for the pastoral minister, particularly in this transitional time when we are still finding our way into the OCF, derives from an appreciation of what this vigil is about. If the use of personal mementos is to find a natural home in the vigil, then they are to be included with moderation. Pastoral ministers must find ways to ensure that their use does not eclipse the whole reason for gathering as a liturgical assembly in this vigil — to be consoled by the Christian remembering of the redeeming word of God.

Does the Rosary Have a Place? The OCF offers two forms of prayer for the vigil: the liturgy of the word and some part of the Office for the Dead.[5] It does not suggest the rosary. However, pastoral sensitivity would suggest that if we take into consideration the spirituality of the bereaved, there are times when this prayer may be appropriate. On the other hand, since the intent of the vigil is to turn to God's word as a source of faith, it is clear that the proclamation of the word of God must be central, no matter what form the vigil takes. The spirituality of the renewed funeral rites is paschal, drawing on the wellspring of sacred scripture rather than on devotional practices. However, although the rosary is not the word of God, it is not entirely unrelated to the scriptures. With its mantra style that allows thoughts to flow freely into the mysteries it contemplates — the mysteries of the life, death and resurrection of Jesus — the rosary may find a place in the period of waking. The time of death is not the time to teach a new way of praying or to be dogmatic and absolutist about our rites. It is often the case that people know no other way of public prayer at this time and, while their familiarity with the rosary is to be respected, this may be an occasion for opening up other possibilities.

If the family's preference is to pray the rosary, then pastoral ministers might gently suggest that the rosary be prayed apart from the vigil rather than instead of it. Unlike the vigil, which presumes an evening hour, the rosary does not require a particular time. Perhaps it could be prayed in the afternoon, especially if a number of elderly people attached to the devotion would be more likely to come then than after dark. The rosary could also be prayed before the vigil, with at least a quarter-hour between the end of the devotion and the beginning of the rite. A parish minister might be the one to lead the rosary, in respect to the piety of the bereaved, although the same minister need not lead both. Providing leaders for the rosary might be part of the ministry of an established parish group, for example, while members of the pastoral ministry team lead the vigil.

To younger people, the rosary is largely unfamiliar and they may not be interested in praying this way. This was the case when Dot, a much-loved mother, grandmother and great-grandmother, died.

At Dot's funeral Mass, her oldest daughter spoke of her as "already sacred to many: awesome, able to empower others to take courage, to recognize their self-worth and to rise to better things." Dot's adult children knew that whatever they did for the vigil would have to be authentic and relevant for the younger generation. Although all were from families of faith, none were churchgoers. To pray the rosary would have no resonance for them. Mary's Magnificat provided the inspiration for how they would shape the vigil celebration, for they saw much in that canticle of praise that was characteristic of Dot's life. In the Magnificat they saw the secret of Dot's inner beauty, a beauty that was loved and respected. For people who knew Dot, something did leap when she came into their presence, just as something leaped in the womb of Elizabeth. The vigil that night was simple. After words of introduction and an opening prayer, the gospel was proclaimed. Several of Dot's grandchildren spoke in memory of her. They told stories of Dot the provider, the joy-giver, the one who reached out to provide with good things, the lover of justice and beauty, the one who loved and respected across faiths, cultures and generations, the one who always encouraged and recognized the good and the beautiful in life. Dot's grandchildren and great-grandchildren knew the gospel, not from the Bible, but from the gospel lived by Dot.

Dot's grandchildren remembered her that night in a way that could be inspired by no other word than the scriptural word and the word of Dot's own living. This was an occasion when the family and the community truly "turned to God's word as the source of faith and hope" (OCF, 56).

What About a Vigil Mass? The OCF offers two forms of prayer for the vigil, a liturgy of the word or a form of the Office for the Dead. It does not suggest eucharist, and yet it seems to be the practice, at least in Australia, and particularly in cases of the death of a priest or a member of a priest's family, to have Mass instead of a liturgy of the word as the vigil celebration. This practice seems to suggest that some members of the community are more deserving than others, with Mass for the more deserving and a liturgy of the word for the less deserving. That question aside, we surely need to explore the wisdom behind the vigil models offered in the OCF.

The title of the ritual book containing this repertoire of rites for funerals is the *Order* of Christian Funerals. There is a deliberate intent behind the way that these rites begin at death and move in a sequential way through to the time of committal. Each rite has its own time and place within the whole, its own integrity, its own particular purpose and action. In a continuum of both familial and public rituals — the vigil and related rites and prayers, the funeral liturgy and the rite of committal — the deceased and the believing community enter into a process of separation. It is a process that ritually allows a constructive negotiation of death and the disorder and confusion brought by death. This process reaches its peak with the central funeral celebration — the funeral liturgy — which, when possible and pastorally desirable, is a celebration of eucharist. Eucharist, as *the* ritual enactment of the paschal mystery, is *the* celebration that expresses the meaning that the death and resurrection of Jesus give to the death of a Christian.

To interrupt this natural flow of rites with a vigil Mass seems to disrupt the whole process. It denies an opportunity for the bereaved to ponder and dwell with death, the opportunity the vigil provides. The funeral Mass asks that the community move on. The practice of a vigil Mass brings up such questions as: Do we understand what vigiling is about? Do we really appreciate the fact that a rich ritual process at the time of death can lead the bereaved into an environment where they can at least begin to deal with the reality of death, and to enter gradually into a journey of separation? Do we really believe that in death there are no distinctions and that no one group within the baptized community is privileged? A necessary aspect of thinking through the ensemble of rites of the OCF is to grasp the fact that we are not engaged in a series of disconnected rituals, but in a whole intentional process through which the bereaved might travel the painful path of leave-taking as they prepare to live in a different relationship with the deceased in the confident hope that the deceased now lives with God.

Adaptation of the Vigil for the Deceased
Two examples of vigil celebrations may serve to illustrate the
flexibility of the vigil.

> *Dympna, a much-loved member of the parish, died at the age of 85.
> An illness during her forties had plunged her into the silence of
> deafness. She had lived in that silence for longer than four decades.
> It seemed right that Dympna's vigil be characterized by silence, so,
> in the silence of the night, a small group from the parish gathered
> with Dympna's relatives to keep vigil in a comfortable room
> adjacent to the main body of the church.*[6] *The paschal candle was
> burning in the center of the room.*
>
> *Two of Dympna's nephews wheeled the coffin into the room. As
> it was placed near the candle, a cantor sang and all repeated: "The
> light of Christ. Thanks be to God." After some moments of silence,
> two other members of her family came forward and ritually
> opened the coffin. The ensuing silence flowered into the words of a
> poem, "Deaf One."*[7] *More silence followed, after which the words
> of the prophet Isaiah were proclaimed: "The Lord GOD has given
> me the tongue of a teacher, that I may know how to sustain the
> weary with a word. Morning by morning he wakens — wakens
> my ear to listen as those who are taught. The Lord GOD opened my
> ear, and I was not rebellious" (Isaiah 50:4 – 5).*
>
> *Family and friends were then invited to remember this "deaf
> one," this woman who heard as a disciple in spite of her deafness.
> Many stories were told, and at times the words of Isaiah were
> called up as a refrain; the same passage brought the remembering
> to a conclusion. Prayers of intercession followed. After a final
> prayer, all came forward to sign or touch Dympna. During the*

*singing of the refrain "In our darkness there is no darkness with you,
O God; the deepest night is clear as the day," the coffin was closed.*

*Kevin's vigil took place in a part of the church that had been
rearranged as a wake chapel. Kevin had committed suicide. For
many reasons his life was full of anguish. He was convinced that
he was a failure, that he was unlovable, that there was no point to
living. He had attempted suicide several times before.*

*Kevin's coffin had been brought to the chapel an hour before the
vigil began, and in that time family and a small group of friends
gathered. As the vigil began, the leader stood and said: "Our
friend Kevin is dead. He had thirty-five years of life with us, many
of which were troubled. He died just two days ago. We gather in
prayer this evening and bring our grief to our compassionate God."
A solo voice sang the first verse of the hymn "Farewell," set to the
plaintive tune FINLANDIA.*

*Farewell! We come to send you on the way
we all must walk, so final, secret, strange.
In wond'ring awe, in grief and hope we pray,
pilgrims of time, to one who does not change . . .
Whose love can lead us through the darkest night
to life and joy in everlasting light.[8]*

*As people began to sing the following verses, Kevin's sister and one
of his friends opened the coffin. The leader invited those present
to mark Kevin with the sign of the cross, the sign with which he was
first marked in baptism.*

*The word of God proclaimed that evening was surrounded
with prayerful silence. The word from the Book of Lamentations
(3:17 – 26) reflected Kevin's anguished life and God's faithfulness
in time of distress. A second proclamation based on John 14:1 – 6[9]*

*was sung. Kevin's restless heart could indeed be still. A time of
remembering Kevin followed, and the word from the Gospel of
John was again sung. Prayers of intercession, a concluding prayer
and a prayer over the mourners were then prayed. The vigil
concluded with a setting of the Nunc Dimittis.*[10]

Office for the Dead

The second vigil model offered in the OCF is some part of the
Office for the Dead. The "some part" offered in the OCF is
Morning Prayer and Evening Prayer, the main parts of the Liturgy
of the Hours. The Liturgy of the Hours is a particular form of
official liturgical prayer sometimes known as the Prayer of the
Church or the Divine Office. The name Liturgy of the *Hours* is a
clear indication that this prayer is a prayer of *time,* intended to be
prayed at the turning points of the day. Since dawn and dusk,
sunrise and sunset, morning and evening, are natural moments of
pause, lending themselves to prayer and reflection, it is not
surprising that the OCF suggests morning and evening as ripe
times for prayer for the dead.

It is at Morning Prayer that the Christian community recalls
"the resurrection of the Lord Jesus, the true light enlightening all
people and the 'sun of justice' 'rising from on high'".[11] Morning
Prayer from the Office for the Dead is a fitting celebration,
enabling the community to "relate the death of the Christian to
Christ's victory over death and affirm the hope that those who
have received the light of Christ at baptism, will share that victory"
(OCF, 350). At Evening Prayer, the community gathers in thanksgiving for the gifts it has received, "to recall the saving works of
redemption and to call upon Christ, the evening star and
unconquerable light" (OCF, 351). When Evening Prayer from the

Office for the Dead is prayed, the community fittingly gives thanks for the life of the deceased and gives praise for the saving death and resurrection of Jesus "who is the joy-giving light and the true source of hope" (OCF, 351).

The Liturgy of the Hours, whether Morning Prayer or Evening Prayer, does not take the shape of word and sacrament familiar to us from our sacramental celebrations. Rather, it has its own specific structure and content, the main elements of which are hymnody, psalmody, proclamation of the word of God and prayer. The richness of the church's Morning and Evening Prayer lies in its core of psalmody, the psalms being songs that cover the whole range of human emotions. The psalms are prayers that provide great comfort and consolation, and often they give us words of lament to say what we otherwise would not dare to say. In the face of the mystery and unreasonableness of death they allow us to give voice to our confusion, grief, bewilderment and anguish. In the psalms of lament, particularly apt for prayer at the time of death, we find words not only to voice our emotions but, as lament turns to praise, to channel our emotions. Psalms of thanksgiving give us words with which we can give thanks for the life of the deceased and for the life, death and resurrection of Jesus, which gives meaning to all our deaths. Psalms of praise, confidence and petition also find a home in this prayer. Thus the Office for the Dead is an occasion for the community to surround the deceased and those who mourn with its prayer of lament, confidence, praise and thanksgiving.

The main difficulty with the church's prayer at morning and evening is that it is largely unfamiliar. Most have not heard of this prayer before. The occasion of death is certainly not the time to spring new ways of prayer on people. If then we hope to use

Morning or Evening Prayer from the Office for the Dead as vigil
prayer, a parish needs to have not only heard about it, but to have
experienced it. Seasonal praying of Morning and Evening Prayer
is an increasing practice. As people become more familiar with it,
realization of its potential for vigil prayer will follow.

Parishes without resident priests may become familiar with this
prayer in their Sunday celebrations. Another opportunity to
reclaim this prayer as the church's prayer might also be on "Father's
day off" — a day when weekday Mass is not possible. In places
where the faithful are only occasionally deprived of the Mass, the
celebration of Morning Prayer might become the alternative to
the more usual communion service at those times when Mass is
not possible.

Catechesis and familiarity with Morning and Evening Prayer
from the Liturgy of the Hours is essential if the potential of the
Office for the Dead is to be realized. As awareness of this prayer
grows, and as people become more familiar with the tradition of
psalmody, Christians will discover a rich source of prayer with
which to enter deeply into their loss in the company of a God who
has the power to turn lament and sorrow into praise.

OFFICE FOR THE DEAD
MORNING AND EVENING PRAYER

❖

Introductory verse

Hymn

Psalmody and silence

Reading and silence

Responsory

Gospel canticle

(Morning Prayer: Canticle of Zechariah;

Evening Prayer: Canticle of Mary)

Intercessions

The Lord's Prayer

Concluding prayer

Dismissal

[Procession to the place of committal,
if Morning Prayer is the central funeral liturgy]

❖

CHAPTER FOUR
TIME TO WELCOME, GIVE THANKS AND BID FAREWELL: THE FUNERAL LITURGY

Central Moment in the Funeral Rites

The funeral liturgy is the "central liturgical celebration of the Christian community for the deceased" (OCF, 128). This is when the community "gathers with the family and friends of the deceased to give praise and thanks to God for Christ's victory over sin and death, to commend the deceased to God's tender mercy and compassion, and to seek strength in the proclamation of the paschal mystery" (OCF, 129). In order for the funeral liturgy to be central, it must be preceded by some things (the vigil and related rites) and followed by something (the committal).

The OCF offers two forms of funeral liturgy: the funeral Mass and the funeral liturgy outside Mass (OCF, 128). The latter includes all the elements of the funeral Mass except the celebration of eucharist. It is intended for use in situations where Mass cannot be celebrated, or when for pastoral reasons a liturgy of the word might be more appropriate.

Both forms of the funeral liturgy are framed by intentional rites of welcome and farewell. Respectively, these are the rite of reception of the body and the rite of final commendation and farewell (which in turn leads to the transfer of the body to the place of committal). The focus is on the body of the deceased — a primary symbol in the OCF.

Time to Welcome: A Baptismal Rite

The community gathers, when possible, at the entrance of the church to receive and welcome the body of the deceased. It is important that this rite not be seen simply as a "curtain raiser" that sets the scene for the "real" action of the Mass. It is in fact a discrete rite with its own integrity, purpose and place in the liturgy. Receiving the body of the deceased is an action by which the "members of the community acknowledge the deceased as one of their own" (OCF, 131), and hold and cherish the deceased in prayer and loving memory for a time before the letting-go asked in the final commendation. As the community assembles to welcome the deceased into its midst for the last time, it does so in the way the deceased in baptism began his or her journey of faith — with candle, water, cross, word, white garment and community. Death for the Christian is a culmination of the pilgrimage of paschal faith that began in baptism.

Ideally, the rite of reception of the deceased is celebrated when the body of the deceased is brought to the church, usually from the funeral home. The OCF presumes that, where possible, the rite of transfer of the body of the deceased to the church or place of committal has already been prayed by the family, presumably at the funeral home; that the family has accompanied the body to the church; and that a pastoral minister representing the local parish community has been with the family through the difficult initial leave-taking. As mentioned in the discussion on the related rites and prayers, it makes good pastoral and ritual sense that the transfer of the body be timed to allow the community to assemble at the church for this communal act of receiving the deceased into its midst for the last time. This is the ideal, but there is often a gap in the ritual process at this point. This will be taken up in more detail below, in the discussion of pastoral concerns.

With Candle, Water, White Garment, Cross,
Word and a Community of Faith

The OCF envisages that the rite of reception take place at the doors of the church. Doorways are places of passage, of entry and exit, of welcome and farewell. This rite is full of action intended to be done around the coffin. The rite is made for gathering, for doing, seeing and responding. If it is to do its work, it must be carried out in a space where such action can be attended to with lavish dignity and grace, a space where the action may be full and participative. This rite would make little pastoral sense if it did not engage the total assembly.[1]

Pastoral awareness suggests that if the entrance to the church does not physically allow for the liturgical action of reception of the body of the deceased, some adaptations may need to be made depending on such circumstances as the size of the funeral assembly and the physical arrangement and sound system of the church. For instance, ministers of hospitality might invite those who arrive before the body to take seats toward the back of the church, advising them that this is where the body of the deceased will be welcomed. Then the assembly would process to the place where the rest of the liturgy will take place during the processional hymn. Another alternative might be that once the people have taken their places, the coffin would be carried (preferably not wheeled — this is a time for human touch) through the assembly to be placed by the paschal candle, in which case the family would follow the coffin. Or, if a parish has a spacious and gracious baptistry, that would be a very fitting place to welcome the body of the deceased, highlighting the connection between water baptism and the baptism of death.

It makes eminent sense to use water from the font in the ritual gesture of sprinkling. If the area allows for the family to stand around the coffin, they too could sprinkle or wash the coffin with water. Just as minimal dabs of water do not belong in baptism, neither do they belong in our funeral rites. In fact, the term "sprinkling" seems unsatisfactory in our rites that involve water. Water scooped up in both hands and cascading onto the coffin is a much stronger symbol. The sound and sight of falling water would contribute greatly to the meaning and fullness of this action.

The clothing of the coffin with the white pall is optional, and not universally familiar. Clothing is a mark of identity. The pall, with its strong baptismal overtones, marks the deceased as belonging to the communion of all the baptized in which all are equal. Yes, Jim could have been buried as a pauper, unclaimed by anyone, but Jim's coffin was clothed with the same white pall that clothes the coffin of every other baptized member of the parish of St. Joseph. The dignified clothing of the coffin with the white pall can be a powerful action. The verb "clothing" suggests that the pall be generous in its size. This rules out the use of a white corporal or purifier or even an altar cloth — these have other uses. Nor should a white stole be used — stoles are part of the vesture of the ordained. They simply are not palls. Only unawareness of the symbolic action of placing the pall on the coffin of the deceased could excuse the use of other cloths.

It is fitting that family members clothe the coffin with the pall in actions that are deliberate and unhurried. They may need to practice so that they can be comfortable with the action. We can learn something from Dympna's funeral.

*Four of Dympna's nieces were named after her. At Dympna's
funeral, these four Dympnas gracefully and lovingly clothed her
coffin with the white pall. Their action was accompanied by
these words: "May Christ who claimed you, Dympna, in baptism,
now enfold you in his love and bring you to eternal life."[2] Some
time after the funeral, as the family was thinking back over those
days, one of the nieces who had always been embarrassed by her
name said that now she loved the name Dympna as she had loved
Dympna herself. She added that if she could live her life with
the patience and acceptance of her aunt, then Dympna's life will
have gained even more meaning and purpose. Clothing the coffin
with the pall had led her to this reflection. In death, Dympna had
become minister and witness.*

The OCF makes provision for the placing of other Christian
symbols — cross, Bible, book of the gospels — once the coffin
is placed. This is optional. There may be some circumstances where
the placing of these symbols would be inappropriate or even
dishonest, particularly if the scriptures or the cross held little or
no obvious place in the life of the deceased. A better approach
might be to use these symbols when it makes sense to do so, when
their use is an honest expression of the Christian life and piety of
the deceased.

The rite of reception requires a well-considered choreography
with a sense of momentum, movement that suits the particular
space in which it is enacted. In many cases, precisely because of the
arrangement of the space, the order of the elements of the rite in
the OCF require rethinking. If the rite cannot take place at the
entrance to the church, or if it will not work to have people turn
to face the back of the church, then it is probably better to begin

with a processional hymn as the coffin is carried into the church by the pallbearers and placed by the paschal candle. After words of greeting and introduction, the actions with water, pall and other Christian symbols would then follow. These symbolic actions and words must be seen and heard. The OCF provides optional texts to be prayed during the gestures of sprinkling and for the placing of other symbols. These are meant to accompany the action, to be spoken and paced so that they are heard clearly, in order to lend meaning to the actions and engage the assembly. Sometimes, music might enrich this rite.

Alternatively, the texts that accompany the actions might be printed in an order of service to be prayed as a dialogue between the presider and the assembly. For example:

Presider: In the waters of baptism,
   N. died with Christ
   and rose with him to new life:
All: May N. now share eternal life with him in glory.

The rite can potentially become quite disjointed, seeming to be a string of unconnected acts and words. The rite needs to feel like a unit, offering a sense that it is leading somewhere. Music is a good way to hold it together. One way to lend unity to the rite would be to sing all but the last stanza of the processional hymn at the procession into the church, with a musical interlude accompanying the placing of Christian symbols once the body is in its place in the assembly. Then, the final stanza of the processional hymn could be sung after the placing of the symbols and just before the opening prayer. Another way to use music in this rite is with a good setting of the second memorial acclamation ("Dying you destroyed our death . . ."), or an antiphon such as "Awake O Sleeper." These are particularly appropriate for the rite of reception. The acclamation or antiphon could be played as one voice proclaims the texts accompanying each action and then sung by all after each action.

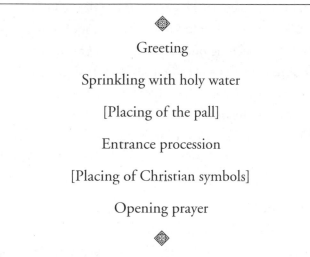

RITE OF RECEPTION OF THE BODY AT CHURCH
[BEFORE THE FUNERAL LITURGY]

Greeting

Sprinkling with holy water

[Placing of the pall]

Entrance procession

[Placing of Christian symbols]

Opening prayer

Pastoral Considerations around the Rite of Reception of the Body
The Arrival of the Body at the Church. The fact that this is a rite of *reception* implies that the body of the deceased is to be brought from somewhere else, and that a community has accompanied it or come together to receive it. Yet this does not always happen, because of the schedules of the funeral directors. A community that is serious about its ministry of care of the dead will ensure that there is always a welcoming presence when the body arrives at the church. This challenges the unthinking practice of dropping off

the body of the deceased like a package, leaving the coffin to wait alone, without ceremony, until people arrive for the funeral.

There might be circumstances when the transfer of the body to the church unavoidably does not coincide with the timing of the funeral liturgy. In that case, the very least called for would be the presence of a group of parishioners to welcome the family and the body on arrival at the church, and to keep prayerful vigil until the funeral liturgy begins. This welcoming of the body may or may not take the form of a full rite of reception, but the presence of a community reaching out in care ensures gracious hospitality in the act of receiving one of its own. If the parish has a wake chapel or spacious baptismal area, then the coffin would have a dignified place to rest until the time of the funeral.

Symbols and Personal Mementos. A statement in the General Introduction to the OCF about the use of Christian and "other symbols" has elicited strong reaction in some circles.

> Only Christian symbols may rest on or be placed near the coffin during the funeral liturgy. Any other symbols, for example, national flags, or flags or insignia of associations, have no place in the funeral liturgy. . . . [They] are to be removed from the coffin at the entrance to the church. They may be replaced after the coffin has been taken from the church. (OCF, 38, 132)

Taken by itself, this statement certainly seems to have a dogmatic and prohibitive tone. Perhaps we need to stand back from the statement to find its underlying wisdom. How might we interpret it and what might be its liturgical and pastoral intent?

It is important to understand the statement in the context of the whole ritual process. The reference to "funeral liturgy" is quite intentional. It is not used to refer loosely to funerals in general, but to refer to that particular central rite — the funeral Mass or funeral liturgy outside Mass — distinct from any of the other rites in the funeral process. This intention becomes clearer in the latter part of the statement about removing "other symbols" before the funeral liturgy with the option of replacing them after.

With the vigil, there was opportunity to dwell with the life and death of the deceased. The funeral liturgy carries a sense of *moving on* to place the life and death of the deceased into a larger, cosmic — Christian — context. This does not imply forgetting the deceased or denying grief, for throughout the funeral liturgy the church remembers the deceased as it prayerfully intercedes for the deceased. The funeral liturgy simply has another main intent: "to give praise and thanks for Christ's victory over sin and death . . . and to seek strength in the proclamation of the paschal mystery" (OCF, 129). In this ritual act of remembering the death and resurrection of Jesus, the gathered community can indeed give thanks and confidently "commend the deceased to God's tender mercy and compassion" (OCF, 129).

The Christian meaning of death and the motivating force of a person's life of faith do not lie in "national flags, or flags or insignia of associations" (OCF, 38), or indeed in other personal mementos. That meaning derives from the death of Jesus issuing into resurrection, enacted in every eucharist.

The statement regarding flags and other insignia of associations is not saying that they are un-Christian, nor that they can have no place in funerals, for they can be replaced on the coffin at the end of the funeral liturgy. It seems then that the intent of this paragraph about "other symbols" is simply to ensure that the Christian focus is central. Its intent is surely to emphasize the importance of a paschal journey begun in baptism and culminating in death. In the rite of reception the deceased is welcomed as one whose *baptism* gave him or her a rightful place in the community, and who now enjoys the company of the communion of saints in heaven and on earth.

The communion of saints is not exactly an association. At this point in the funeral rite, while still mindful of the life journey of the deceased, history passes into mystery, the mystery with the power to embrace the deceased's history and to transform death into life. If this paschal focus were to be subsumed by any other, the integrity and intent of the funeral liturgy and its place in the ritual process would be lost.

The rite of reception is probably when the request for inclusion of personal mementos or other symbols (OCF, 38) is most likely to collide with the use of baptismal symbols. The collision is particularly likely if it has not been possible to have a vigil service. Pastoral ministers must be sensitive to the need for funerals to be occasions for articulating and hearing the life story of the deceased and hearing the story of the grief of the bereaved. There is nothing worse than a generic funeral or a funeral that separates faith and life.

It is easy to say that the use of personal mementos belongs in the vigil. And of course they find a natural home there. Once again, the pastoral minister must remember that the time to teach what our funeral rites are about is not when people are grieving and in shock. At the same time, the very reason that the Christian community gathers for this funeral is that the deceased was Christian. This is an aspect of the story of the deceased that the community needs to remember — the story of his or her faith journey, where it began and where it finds fulfilment. There is a world of difference between memento and symbol, and the funeral liturgy is not the place for indulging in nostalgia. Our repertoire of Christian symbols — water, light, cross, word, bread and wine and the assembly itself — are the containers and bearers of a faith that is grounded in the paschal mystery. Personal mementos cannot do this particular work.

So how might a minister deal with this question with pastoral awareness and sensitivity, and at the same time with respect for the intent of the rite of reception? The following guidelines might be helpful:

1. There is almost unlimited scope within the vigil for speaking of the deceased and for reflecting on memories. The vigil seems to be the natural context for this to occur, since it is celebrated in the in-between time that readily lends itself to telling the stories.

2. If mementos are used at the funeral liturgy, and this may be so if there has not been a vigil, one must ensure that the intentional and inherently Christian nature of the rite of reception of the body is not obscured; it is because the deceased is Christian that the community comes together to do the work that Christians must do in the face of death. The presider might incorporate the remembering into the words of welcome and introduction through the requested mementos. They could be arranged in a prepared space, after which the presider might invite the assembly to recall another story — the story of the faith life of the deceased — and then proceed with the sprinkling and clothing of the coffin.

3. Pastoral sensitivity and awareness of what our rites mean need to guide the use of personal mementos. Pastoral ministers cannot afford to be dogmatic at the time of death.

The practice of using personal mementos in our liturgies for funerals is relatively recent. If our funeral rites stop short of inviting the bereaved to see beyond this life that has ended, then we are in danger of indulging in nostalgia or premature canonization. After all, liturgy is never meant to leave us where we are, but rather to lead us on. If the only point of gathering is to tell the story of the deceased's prestigious football career, using all the memorabilia, then why not gather at the football stadium? We went through a time when anything could be presented in "offertory processions" at Mass, and it is only in recent years that a more informed appreciation of what the procession with eucharistic gifts is all about has been reflected in our practice. At this early stage in the implementation of the OCF, perhaps we are at a similar point. If so, the situation may right itself as time goes on.

Parishes will find it valuable to think deeply about the rite of reception. Where is it best done, given the architecture and furnishings of our churches? How is the family to be involved? How shall this rite be attended to so that it does not become a series of unrelated elements? How can the whole assembly be partici-pants and not just simply spectators? Would it be worthwhile to do part of the rite of reception at the vigil and other elements at the funeral liturgy where more of the community might be present? What happens with this rite of welcome and reception if there are requests from the family to use personal mementos, particularly if there has not been a vigil service? What difference would it make if there were no rite of reception?

Time to Give Thanks: Word and Sacrament

The OCF sees eucharist as integral to this central ritual moment of taking leave of a Christian who has died. Eucharist, the narrative act of our faith, the narrative that proclaims the passage of Jesus through death to resurrection, eucharist is the sacrament that speaks most powerfully about the meaning of death. It is the paschal mystery, enacted in eucharist, that enables Christians to begin to make sense of death and to see meaning in death's mystery. This ritual moment of the funeral liturgy invites the bereaved to experience more explicitly the hope and consolation that emerge from our basic Christian belief in the cross and resurrection. The way in which a parish celebrates its Sunday eucharist will carry through to the funeral liturgy. If Sunday Mass is celebrated with grace and thought, our funeral rites will be mindful and inspiring.[3] If our Sunday liturgies are thoughtless, our funeral liturgies will be thoughtless as well.

In word and sacrament the community proclaims the mystery of our faith. In the proclamation of the word of God the bereaved have the opportunity to hear God speaking to them in their pain and loss and to respond to God in their grief. In the midst of the disorder and confusion brought about by death the assembly hears that God's design is of a world where suffering and death are not the final word. In the dying and rising of Jesus, death with its sting and apparent victory is eradicated. Death indeed is defeated.

Careful selection of readings and attentive proclamation ensure that the liturgy takes on an appropriately personal note. The selection of readings will take into account the life, and the faith life, of the deceased, the emotional and spiritual needs of the family and friends of the bereaved, and the circumstances of death. Regrettably, some families of the deceased are content to leave this selection to the priest or pastoral minister. And yet the perusal of the readings in order to make the selections can be beneficial for the bereaved, a rich occasion for remembrances of the deceased.

At the funeral liturgy, the homily is integral. As part of the liturgy of the word, one of the functions of the homily is to ensure that the "members of the community . . . receive consolation and strength to face the death of one of their members with a hope nourished by the saving word of God" (OCF, 27). Ill-prepared sermons or mere summaries of the deceased's life cannot do this work. Worse are homilies in which the homilist pretends to know the person who has died, or homilies that subject the assembly to a set of clichés. If the person giving the homily has spent time with the family, listening to the story of the deceased and to the family's grief, if the word of God has been carefully chosen to reflect or somehow speak of the life of the deceased or the grief of the bereaved, then much of the homily material is in hand. While the homily is not to be purely a eulogy (OCF, 27) — that is, extolling words focusing entirely on the deceased — the occasion demands that the life of the deceased be incorporated into the homily; it demands too that the grief of the bereaved be voiced.

The homily is not a time to preach how life should be lived, to moralize about the living-out of Christian faith, to engage in dry discourses on the meaning of death, or to outline how one should or should not feel about death. Nor is it an occasion to offer a quick and easy word that seeks to soften the reality of loss, or to interpret Christian hope as mere optimism. Gospel hope acknowledges that "losses are losses and ends are ends [and] that is the context in which hope must operate."[4] Gospel hope names the reality of grief and irretrievable loss, and in the midst of that loss offers the assurance that no amount of pain and suffering can separate us from the God who is with us in our suffering. In offering a faithful response to death, and a hope nourished by the word of God, the homily can be a great grace for all.

With such hope, the ministering assembly can indeed turn to God in confidence and trust as it intercedes on behalf of the deceased and as it places the human condition before God. This assembly has come together on a specific occasion — the death of a Christian — the death of one who held a place in the lives of family and friends and in the life of the faith community. Given this, the prayers of intercession take on a different focus than that of the usual Sunday prayers. So the community prays "for the deceased, all the dead, for the family and all who mourn and for all in the assembly" (OCF, 29). The prayers of intercession are yet another opportunity for the funeral liturgy to become personal. Springing from the meeting of liturgy and life, having their origin in the life of the deceased, in the sickness and death of the deceased, in our own confrontation with mortality, these prayers give opportunity for the assembly to stand with the bereaved and hold the deceased before God in prayer.

It is with the memory of the deceased and the memory of God's promises that the assembly can approach the eucharistic table and find in sacrament the fulfillment of hope in these promises. It is around the table that the assembly gives praise and thanks to God for the mystery in which lies the source of their hope — Christ's victory over sin and death. Strengthened by this hope, nourished by the sharing of bread and cup, the meal that foreshadows the heavenly banquet, the assembly can then stand with the bereaved in a rite that invites them to bid farewell and entrust their loved one "to the tender and merciful embrace of God" (OCF, 146).

Time to Bid Farewell and Commend: Beginning to Let Go
With the rite of final commendation and farewell, the body of the deceased again becomes the focus. Having welcomed the deceased in the rite of reception of the body, the assembly now directs its attention to bidding farewell and letting go. This is an action

toward which the funeral liturgy and indeed the whole ritual process has been moving, bringing the bereaved yet closer to the moment of final leave-taking. It is charged with emotion as the bereaved prepare to accompany their loved one to his or her final place of rest.

This point in the liturgy is neither the first nor last moment of farewell for the bereaved, but this is when the funeral rite invites them to bid their farewell in an intentional and public ritual act. Those who mourn know that they are not left to do this alone, but that they do so in the presence of a community which has been with them from the outset of this journey of grief and loss. Strengthened in the celebration of eucharist, and in the midst of this ministering assembly of support and prayer, the bereaved know that they can safely and confidently hand the deceased over to God and entrust him or her to God's care. It is time to let go, in the knowledge that God will not abandon us in our grief.

The rite of final commendation and farewell occurs at the end of the funeral liturgy, unless it is to be celebrated later at the place of committal.[5] Like the rite of reception, it has its own integrity, purpose and place in the ritual process. It is important that this rite not be seen as a mere appendage "tacked on" to the end of Mass. This can happen if the presiding minister "finishes" the Mass with the final blessing and dismissal and then "begins again" with the final commendation and farewell.

Following the prayer after communion, the rite of final commendation and farewell begins with an invitation that draws attention to the immediacy of leave-taking and climaxes as the assembly sings its farewell. The rite does not conclude with a final blessing and dismissal, but with another invitation, this time, to continue the journey by accompanying the deceased to his or her place of final rest.

Farewell in Sign and Song

Like the rite of reception, the rite of final commendation and farewell is intended for action — for seeing, doing, hearing, smelling, feeling, gathering — and thus presents another challenge to pastoral ministers. It must command the attention of the whole assembly and engage them in its action. If the rite is not given the full attention that enables it to do its work, the final commendation and farewell can be simply a time when people get themselves and their belongings together to leave the church.

The rite is brief and poignant, inviting the assembly to bid its farewell in both sign and song and to commend the deceased to the care of God and the company of saints. This rite can easily be misunderstood, particularly since water and incense are used as signs of farewell, whereas at the same point in our old funeral rites they were signs of purification and absolution. The OCF suggests that these signs be used as the assembly sings its farewell. If the song is truly a song of farewell and commendation, then water and incense have an accompanying word and a context in which they can do their work of signifying the farewell of the community.

The OCF authorized for Canada provides two spoken texts that may accompany the actions with which the assembly signs its farewell. The formula that accompanies the action of sprinkling with water helps us to understand that this is not about absolution. The sprinkling is a baptism of death and in these waters the deceased is plunged into the fullness of life in Christ:

In baptism, N. shared in the death and resurrection of Christ.
May he/she be welcomed into the glory of eternal life.
(OCF [Canada], 342)

Lavish use of water is called for. The assembly needs to see and
hear the water. However, if water has been used as part of the rite
of reception, it is better not to repeat its use at the rite of final
commendation and farewell. In that case, incense is to be used as
the farewell sign.

The assembly needs to see and smell clouds of incense. Generous
and graceful use of incense at this moment also supports the
assembly's action of farewell and commendation. The incensing
must be done thoroughly and mindfully, to make clear the sense
of circling the deceased in a touching gesture of respect and honor.
The accompanying words from the Canadian OCF are helpful:

As a sign of respect for our brother/sister, N.
we let this incense rise to God,
who has called him/her to share in his glory.
(OCF [Canada], 342)

Before the deceased is finally laid to rest, time is given for the
community to express its faith and to sing its farewell. This song
of farewell is the central element and climax of the rite of final
commendation and farewell. It is hard to do this song well; it
presents opportunities and challenges.

The more difficult question about this song seems to involve
appropriateness. What is appropriate for this particular group of
people who will sing this song? What is appropriate for this
particular occasion of death? Is it to be a song of faith? To whom is
this song addressed? How do farewell and faith meet in this song?
Is this the time to sing the deceased's favorite song? Must the words

of the song be an explicit expression of farewell? Is this song to
be a prayer? If so, is it to be the prayer of the assembly or a prayer
voiced on behalf of the deceased?

The texts suggested in the ritual book are a mixed selection.
On the one hand, they are chosen from ancient responsories and
formulas, and the best of them is "Saints of God." This text
certainly offers a sense that we can be confident in handing over
the deceased into the care of God, and confident that he or she will
receive warm and eager welcome from the company of the angels
and the saints. On the other hand, some other texts contain
sentiments of shame, sinfulness and need for deliverance that are
hardly consonant with a spirit of confident farewell and commendation. But perhaps this uneven selection is simply indicative
of the paucity of texts available and suitable for this moment of
farewell. This points to our need for strong poetry that can carry
the faith of the Christian community and its farewell to one of its
members, as well as the emotion of this farewell.

The parish repertoire of songs of farewell need not be large. In
fact, one or two might do. These songs of farewell need not consist
of many stanzas. The right song is simple enough for all to sing,
and poignant enough to voice the assembly's farewell to one of its
own. *Farewell* is our clue about how this song is to function. This
idea calls into question many of the songs that have been used
at this moment. If the song is the farewell of the assembly, perhaps
this means that this is not the occasion to sing the deceased's
favorite song — even if it is a hymn.

It is important that we sing at this powerful moment. It is often
said that this is too difficult a time for song, that people are too
choked up with emotion to sing. But we all know the power of
raised voices in a ministering assembly as it surrounds the bereaved
with its song of faith and support.

The story is told of a monastery in France that stopped the practice of chanting, for a newly-appointed abbot was convinced that in this day and age chant served no useful purpose. Within a short time, seventy out of the ninety monks complained of fatigue. It was only after several months that a physician suggested that the monks resume their usual chanting schedule. Within five months, almost all the monks regained their health and vigor, and resumed their usual demanding work schedule.[6]

The title of the work from which this story is taken, *Learning to Use the Sound That Heals,* has significance for those who fear that the moment of farewell and commendation is too difficult a time for people to sing. Music is integral to our funeral rites. Music allows the community "to express convictions and feelings that words alone may fail to convey" (OCF, 30). The physical use of the human voice holds a power to heal the human spirit (and in the case of the French monks, a power to heal the body) and to release tensions. If there is one moment that calls out for song in the funeral liturgy, it is the rite of final commendation and farewell.

After the assembly bids farewell in sign and song, the rite concludes with the prayer of commendation, in which the assembly entrusts the deceased to God (OCF, 175). Two prayers are provided. The first seems to be more commonly used. The second is strikingly simple in its acknowledgment of death, and therein lies its strength:

> To you, O Lord, we commend the soul of N. your servant;
> in the sight of this world he/she is now dead;
> in your sight may he/she live forever. . . . (OCF, 175B)

This rite, and thus the whole of the funeral liturgy, does not end with a final blessing and dismissal, as noted earlier, but with an invitation to accompany the body of the deceased in procession to the place of committal (OCF, 176) where the "community will assist the mourners as they complete their care for the deceased and lay the body to rest" (OCF, 213).

The song at this point in the funeral liturgy is intended to function as a processional, since the assembly and mourners will continue their prayer and their care as they take the deceased to another place. The OCF understands this procession also on the level of faith, as it "mirrors the journey of human life as a pilgrimage to God's kingdom of peace and light, the new and eternal Jerusalem" (OCF, 148). The texts provided for this processional song in the rite have long held a place in our funeral rites. The most time-honored sings of union in the great communion of saints, "May the angels lead you into paradise." Fine musical settings of this antiphon are available. Several psalm texts are also provided, and there is liberty to sing other suitable songs. The choice of music for this procession to the place of committal depends on such things as circumstances of death, the life of the person who has died, the faith life of the deceased and the nature of the funeral assembly. However, whatever is sung should have the sense of moving on, reinforcing the invitation to accompany the deceased to the place of committal and final leave-taking.

FINAL COMMENDATION AND FAREWELL

Invitation to prayer

Silence

[Signs of farewell]

Song of farewell

Prayer of commendation

Procession to the place of committal

Pastoral Considerations around the Funeral Liturgy

But Never Any Kind of Eulogy. This matter can incite negative reactions. But note that this statement is part of the OCF's discussion of the funeral homily. "A brief homily based on the readings should always be given at the funeral liturgy, but never any kind of eulogy" (OCF, 141). This statement is not so much about eulogies *per se.* Its intent is to highlight the purpose and nature of the funeral homily, and to ensure that the assembly be nourished with this source of grace and consolation.

Since one of the underlying themes throughout the OCF is attentiveness to the grief of the bereaved and to the circumstances of the life and death of the deceased, this statement surely does not say that narration of the life of the deceased has no part in the funeral liturgy. Nor does it seem to be the intent of the OCF that "Jesus-talk" happens at homily time and talk of the deceased must wait until later, when a member or friend of the family speaks in remembrance of the deceased before the riteof final commendation and farewell begins. The life and death of the deceased must have a place in the funeral liturgy, indeed, in the funeral homily. But the word of God, which has the power to lift the experience of death into a greater dimension than the human story, is paramount. Part of the work of the homilist is to speak a word inspired by the scriptural word that confronts the ultimate reality of death, that in turn offers to the bereaved the community's hope in the resurrection, and that helps the assembly to understand that the mystery of the death and resurrection of Jesus is indeed operative in the life and death of the deceased. The word that embraces the faith story of the Christian community cannot remain unheard. At homily time, words that speak only of the deceased can trivialize the whole purpose of the Christian funeral and can diminish this moment of grace for the assembly. In other words, the homily is not to be a eulogy.

Speaking in Remembrance of the Deceased. Before the rite of final commendation and farewell begins, a friend or family member may speak in remembrance of the deceased, thus paying a final tribute to the deceased before the assembly bids its farewell. This moment of speaking publicly of the deceased in the past tense, in the presence of the body as the time of final leave-taking draws closer, can be a last opportunity to hold on to the deceased before letting go. If this opportunity is taken it must be seen as part of the ritual. It is not "time out" from the liturgy. This is an intense moment, for the community knows that after this brief time of ritualized remembering — and it *is* ritualized — the deceased will be taken to his or her place of rest.

The nature of this optional point in the ritual process demands that the words spoken in honor of the deceased be well-prepared and brief. This does not seem to be the time for multiple speeches, for the moment is too intense and the finality of leave-taking too imminent. Nor does it seem to be the occasion for anecdotes or biographical accounts of personal relationships with the deceased. While the memories that people bring to this funeral will be mixed and cannot all be voiced in this *ritualized* remembering, this moment, in which the deceased is once again raised to the corporate memory of the community, must be honest and real. The deceased is honored for all his or her strengths and weaknesses — and most of us are a mix of saint and sinner. The bereaved and all those gathered must be able to recognize the deceased in these words spoken in his or her remembrance. Pretense or avoidance have no part in this ritualized remembering.

The OCF is not unintentional in its avoidance of the word "eulogy" at this point. How often have we heard "funeral eulogies" that idealize the dead person to the point of premature canonization? And we know that this is not real. The intent of the rite is not to exclude words of praise for the deceased — the essence of eulogy — but perhaps it is in the interest of ritual honesty that the rite calls for this avoidance of eulogistic thinking and language. Pastoral ministers are challenged to assist those who speak to name the life of the deceased as it was. There are cases where particular circumstances of a person's life or death need to be named. To avoid such naming or to succumb to pretense certainly does not assist those who are grieving. If we cannot be honest in our prayer, where can we be honest? After all, "the Christian believes that human life, however paralyzed, however dark, however compromised, perverted, marginalized or smashed up, has been taken up into the life of God."[7]

While the invitation to speak in remembrance of the deceased is a welcome inclusion in our new funeral rites, it does carry with it a certain redundancy. Surely the whole of the ritual process is about that remembrance. A homily that is attentive to the grief of those present and that catches up the life of the deceased, relating it to the death and resurrection of Jesus, functions as powerful remembrance of the deceased. One wonders if there is further need for someone to speak that remembrance if the homily has done its work. There may well be occasions when this speaking in remembrance needs to happen, but this element of the OCF invites further reflection and discussion. It is, after all, optional.

CHAPTER FIVE
TIME TO TAKE LEAVE:
THE RITE OF COMMITTAL

Come Back Here and Bury This Man!

George's funeral took place on a sweltering midsummer afternoon. As the graveside service was nearing its end, people began to move away, out of the heat and toward their air-conditioned cars. But the priest, well-known for his crustiness, ordered: "Come back here and bury this man!"

Their work was unfinished and they were ordered to see it through. No such command was necessary at the graveside service of Henri Nouwen, renowned spiritual writer and member of the L'Arche Daybreak Community in Richmond Hill, Ontario. Of his burial, the *National Catholic Reporter* wrote:

> One hundred family members, friends and members of his L'Arche Daybreak Community stood in the cold around the grave praying and singing as Nouwen's body was returned to the earth. All embraced each other in a large circle around the grave as we prayed the Lord's Prayer. Then each person, beginning with Laurent Nouwen, Nouwen's 93-year-old father, shoveled a pile of wet dirt into the grave. "Sleep well," one of the L'Arche members said. "We'll see you soon."[1]

Here was the work of care of the deceased seen through to its end. Henri's friends indeed committed him to the earth in an honest act that spoke of separation and finality. The scene was earthy, messy and totally devoid of any denial of the harsh reality of death. "Earth to earth, ashes to ashes, dust to dust" was palpable. It was a far cry from the sanitized return to the earth increasingly seen today.

Joel's father was to be laid to rest. When the family and other mourners arrived at the graveside, the floral tributes were neatly arranged at one side of the grave, near the mound of earth covered with artificial grass. Chairs were just as neatly arranged, theater style, under a delicately-colored canopy that provided shade from the sun. When the time came for the act of committal, the coffin was discreetly and smoothly lowered into the grave, but just below ground level. After the blessing over the mourners, a trellis of flowers was moved into place to cover the top of the coffin. The family was then offered cool drinks.

Harshness, starkness, the sign of an open grave — all were disguised in a pretense that denied the reality of committal and separation. The grave as a sign of hope was robbed of its power by its sweet-smelling floral mask. Equally robbed was the sign of lowering the coffin deep into the earth, that repository for our dead which has such place of honor in our Catholic tradition. Meanwhile, the thing that the mourners went to the cemetery to do — to commit the body of the deceased to the earth or the elements — was left to be completed by the anonymous employees of the cemetery. The coffin, suspended over the hole, spoke little of a return to the earth. This regrettable practice is only one small step removed from leaving the coffin suspended unceremoniously over the grave until family and friends have departed.

The graveside service for Henri Nouwen says so much about the essence of the committal rite. Friends and family, not cemetery employees, returned Henri's body to the earth as they gathered in prayer around the gaping hole that was to receive his body. How honestly death and its separation were confronted as they shoveled the wet dirt into the grave; it was a confrontation that their Christian hope enabled them to bear. The words spoken by one of the group that day — "Sleep well, Henri; we'll see you soon!" — were a profound expression of the mystery that Henri was now in the company of the communion of saints awaiting the day of "the glory of the resurrection" (OCF, 206).

At the conclusion of the funeral liturgy, the ministering assembly of prayer is invited to continue its work of consolation and care of the deceased in accompanying their deceased brother or sister to the place of rest. At this site of final rest, a sacred site, the community commits the body of the deceased to the earth or to the elements and at the same time lovingly commits him or her to the company of saints. Throughout the funeral rites, the church has been with the bereaved and the deceased in prayer. Now in this final ritual of leave-taking, which explicitly "marks the separation in this life of the mourners from the deceased" (OCF, 213), the church is present again as a ministering assembly of prayer to assist the bereaved in a powerful act of letting go. A sense of finality characterizes the committal. In this potentially traumatic moment the church proclaims yet again its paschal faith:

> Through this act [of committal] the community of faith proclaims that the grave or place of interment, once a sign of futility and despair, has been transformed by means of Christ's own death and resurrection into a sign of hope and promise. (OCF, 209)

The rite of committal is intended to be celebrated wherever and whenever the disposition of the body is to occur — at the grave, tomb, crematorium, even at sea. The very nature of the rite demands that it be confronting, and that it be celebrated with an integrity and honesty that faces the reality of separation. The growing practice of holding a pseudo-committal rite outside the church that is followed by the hearse driving off into the distance on a lone journey to the final resting place of the deceased is unacceptable. A committal by proxy is absurd. The family and friends have shared the journey of life with the deceased; the death of this one whom they have loved demands that they share the journey of death through to its bitter end of separation. There is nothing more confronting in this separation than standing by as the coffin is lowered into the waiting earth or seeing it go in toward the furnace.

The rite of committal is meant to assist the family and close friends in this difficult moment of letting go. It is not a long rite; in fact it is stark in its brevity. At this place, all that remains is for the body to be committed to the earth or to the elements. The rite begins with a short invitation, a scripture verse and a prayer over the place of committal, whose intent is to prepare the family and friends for the act of committal that they are about to do. That action of committal is the high point of this rite. Like all liturgical actions it needs to be done with strength and dignity. This key moment comes after the prayer of committal or at the end of the whole rite. If it is done after the committal prayer — and this seems the better place for it — it seems appropriate that it be done in a prayerful silence befitting this stark action. This might also be the better time for a gesture of leave-taking, such as throwing a handful of earth into the grave; if this gesture is left until the end of the rite, it seems to be separated from the act of committal itself.

The actual committal of the body "expresses the full significance of the rite" (OCF, 209), and the point is that the body is committed and that the action is completed while the family and friends are gathered at the place of rest. Committal is committal, and that means separation of the mourners from the deceased (OCF, 213). It is crucial that the mourners experience this moment as separation, with finality accompanying it.

Once the body of the deceased has been committed, the rite fittingly concludes with prayers of intercession for the deceased and the mourners, and a prayer over the people. The OCF suggests that there may be a song to conclude. Perhaps this could be a short antiphon or refrain, such as a setting of "Eternal Rest," or a blessing that asks God to bless and keep the deceased and give him or her peace.

Some sign or gesture of final leave-taking is encouraged. The practice of throwing a handful of earth into the grave, a vestige of the physical work of filling in the grave, can be a powerful sign that continues the symbolism of burial and expresses the finality of the moment. It also acknowledges the fact that we are people of the earth, and in being returned to the earth the deceased returns to God. A growing practice in Western funerals is to place flowers in the grave. While flowers also are of the earth, this gesture seems a little weaker. One might question whether this is yet another form of masking the harshness of death.

Isobel was a much-loved grandmother and many tears were shed at her funeral. At the end of the rite of committal, as people were preparing to leave the cemetery, David, one of her adult grandsons, anonymous behind his black sunglasses, sat with head in hands for several minutes on the mound of earth beside her grave. When he stood up he sidled over to the grave, oblivious to the presence of anyone else. He pawed at the ground with his foot. He had work to do. After some time he walked to where the floral tributes had been laid, picked a flower, tossed it into Isobel's grave and walked away.

David couldn't quite pick up a handful of that pawed-at earth, but it was clear that he needed to make some gesture of leave-taking. At least the employees of the funeral home did not provide clean white sand or sanitized potting soil in a plastic bucket, or worse, in a respectable earth-dispenser looking like a pepper grinder. That must be resisted. Death and the act of committal are not respectable or nice, and there seems little sense in this gesture of farewell if the soil is not picked up, touched, handled, felt and allowed to fall — even thud — onto the coffin.

> Buddhist funeral practice might also teach us something:
> The coffin is lowered and the mourners throw flowers and
> some earth into the grave. They then wait until the grave
> is filled and the head of the family places the flowers over
> the mound. In the case of cremation, the head of the family
> will accompany the coffin (where permitted) to the point of
> cremation and then will push the coffin into the furnace.[2]

Committal by Cremation

For more than twenty years, the practice of committal of the body of the deceased by burning has been a canonical option for Catholics in some places. However, given the stigma that it has carried in the past, cremation for some is still probably a confusing issue. The only caveat that the church has included in its statements legitimating cremation is that it not be chosen for anti-Christian motives.[3] Perhaps one difficulty lies in attitudes that see a corpse as human remains, but cremated remains as only ashes. The ashes are not the body — that is clear. But surely both are evidence of the passing nature of the body and of the destructiveness of physical death, the ashes being the result of an accelerated process of decomposition. On this issue, one author writes:

> Catholic tradition, of course, regards fire, like the earth, as an appropriate and reverent disposition of sacramental and other sacred things. Burning has been the recommended way of dealing with sacred objects no longer in use. Both the earth burial . . . and cremation . . . of a body lead to the same ultimate visible material remains: bone fragments.[4]

The OCF reflects the theology and the longstanding tradition of burying the body of the deceased in a grave or tomb. However, because of a number of contemporary cultural influences, cremation is becoming more and more part of Catholic practice. A recent reflection of the National Conference of Bishops of the United States wisely advises:

> While promoting the values that underlie our preference for burial of the body, we must exercise sensitive pastoral judgment concerning the choice that [a percentage] of our people are making in favor of cremation. Economic, geographic, ecological, or family factors on occasion make the cremation of a body the only feasible choice.[5]

The assumption of the OCF is that the cremation, like earth burial, is ordinarily to take place after the funeral liturgy. This is indicative of the church's preference that the body of the deceased be present at its funeral rites, "since the presence of the body most clearly brings to mind the life and death of the person."[6] The liturgical rite in the OCF that accompanies cremation is the same as the rite accompanying earth burial or any form of committal to the elements. The prayer over the place of committal would use option C (see OCF, 218). In the prayer of committal, the words "to be cremated" would replace "to the earth." For ease of use, some conferences of bishops have published committal orders of service that may be used with cremation, some in outline form and others in the form of a complete text. These are not new rites, but easy-to-use arrangements of the normative rite of committal that incorporate the modifications intended for cremation.[7]

One of the criticisms made of cremation is abruptness: If you cannot accompany the body to the crematorium, the rite just seems to stop, not come to a conclusion. The OCF provides the option of a rite that combines the rite of final commendation and farewell with the rite of committal. There may be occasions, particularly if the cremation was not preceded by a funeral liturgy, when pastoral ministers might suggest this option. But when a funeral liturgy is celebrated, it would conclude with the prayer after communion followed by the invitation to take the deceased to the place of committal — even if that is the crematorium.

If the option for cremation is taken, presuming that it takes its natural place in the ritual process — vigil for the deceased, funeral liturgy, rite of committal — there is need for a subsequent liturgical rite on the occasion of the final disposition of the ashes. This later rite follows the usual outline for the rite of committal, with option C for the prayer over the place of committal, and the special prayer provided for the committal of ashes (OCF, 406/3) in the Additional Texts in the OCF.[8]

The "No-Fuss" One-Service Funeral

A growing trend associated with cremation is the funeral directors' "no-fuss" offer for an all-in-one service at the crematorium. The argument is that it's cheaper; it gets things over with so people can get back to their lives "and live happily ever after." There is the earth burial equivalent to this — "Just show up at the chapel at the funeral home or cemetery for a few prayers, and we'll take care of the rest." The situation is more serious with such scandalously crude offers as the equivalent of "early bird specials" — crematorium services scheduled in the off-peak hours at reduced costs. Clearly, such market-driven offers are on a collision course with the theological and pastoral vision of the OCF, as well as its liturgical vision enacted in a ritual process.

These marketing ploys raise the question of why we have funerals in the first place. If they are only about disposal, then the few-prayers model is sufficient and the process might well be shortened in the interests of time and economics. But is it acceptable? Can the Catholic community be satisfied with such a minimalist approach to its work in the face of death? Can it be satisfied to hand over this work to convenient experts?

Pastorally, psychologically and liturgically, a one-service funeral can ask too much of the bereaved, of the human spirit and of the ritual. This is so regardless of whether the form of committal is cremation or earth burial. The funeral is about more than disposal of remains. While not expected to resolve and complete the work of grief, the funeral is integrally related to grieving; and grieving is a process to be negotiated over time. The OCF embodies a ritual process that begins at death and moves from the time of initial shock and adjustment to the moment of leave-taking and final separation. The gradual onward movement through the process allows the bereaved time to dwell with death and with the memories of the deceased and to negotiate the fact that the loved one is now a lifeless corpse. The movement also provides the necessary opportunity for the bereaved to hear and reflect on the word of God that proclaims that in this death there is life, to give praise and thanks to God for the mystery which gives meaning to this death and all our deaths, and to begin a process of farewell which will culminate in the final leave-taking. It seems to be too much for a single ritual to carry all of this, and it may also be too much for the human spirit to move through all this in the space of one ritual moment. And the church requires time, time to tell its own story of death and resurrection which is the Christian source of consolation. The ritual process of the OCF calls the ecclesial community to gather and re-gather during this emotionally laden time and in doing so to surround and re-surround the bereaved and the deceased with its prayer. A single service can be so burdened, asking of the bereaved work of such intensity that the experience of a community of consolation might barely be palpable.

It is easy to be tempted by some of the attractive offers made today, and pastoral ministers must be aware of the issues involved and of what values are being compromised.

Immediate Cremation and Immediate Disposal

Another set of problems has emerged with another trend — the practice of cremation immediately after death followed by immediate disposal.[9] In such cases, there is usually no form of prayerful recognition of death before the removal of the body from the place of death to the crematorium. And later, after the final disposal of the ashes, there may or may not be a "memorial Mass" or service.

To be sure, cremation is a more economical means of disposition of the body, but this does not demand that the deceased be whisked away like a sack of rotten potatoes as soon as possible after death, deprived of the presence of a community of prayer and consolation. Surely our Catholic belief in the dignity and sacramentality of the human creature demands reverent care of the body in death. We have a faith that enables the believer to find the full meaning of a life beyond death. We believe that the deceased has had an ecclesial identity and that the event of death is a summons to the rest of the ecclesial community to gather as a praying assembly. In situations where immediate cremation and disposal may be considered, pastoral ministers must be aware of values and beliefs evidenced in that practice that are inconsistent with Catholic faith.

If the option for immediate cremation is taken, the very least that is called for is some form of prayerful recognition of death before the body is removed. This allows the opportunity for the bereaved to enter into the immediacy of death and its consequences, and for the church to be present in its ministry of consolation. There are models in the OCF from which inspiration might be drawn. Perhaps an adapted form of prayers after death or the vigil for the deceased combined with some elements of the rite of final commendation and farewell could be encouraged. Such prayer would at least allow the bereaved an opportunity to acknowledge that death has happened, and thus to enter into a time when Christian faith might be brought to bear in some way on this life that has ended.

Immediate cremation means that we no longer have a body; we have ashes. Yet the rites of the OCF are designed around the assumption and the clear preference that at each of the public liturgical rites the body, in the form of the corpse, is present. There are certain times when both texts and actions focus specifically on a body. Currently, there is no universal provision for a funeral liturgy in the presence of cremated remains, but Canada has had an indult to so do since 1984. The United States received an indult in 1997 to use a text confirmed by the Holy See.[10]

The United States' *Appendix: Cremation* recommends that cremation occur after the funeral liturgy and the rite of final commendation and farewell. It provides an alternative form of dismissal. After the cremation, the rite of committal is celebrated when the ashes are buried.

If, however, cremation *and* committal take place before the funeral liturgy, "the Prayers After Death and the Vigil for the Deceased may be adapted as necessary and appropriate and used before the Funeral Liturgy. The Rite of Committal with Final Commendation may also be celebrated at that time" (OCF, U.S. Appendix 422), using an alternative form for the words of committal provided. After the committal comes the funeral liturgy, with prayers that do not make mention of honoring or burying the body. The rite of final commendation is omitted (since it has already happened), and the Mass ends in the usual way, with blessing and dismissal. The funeral liturgy outside of Mass ends with a blessing and dismissal after the Lord's Prayer.

When the funeral liturgy is celebrated in the presence of the cremated remains, the U.S. *Appendix* says:

> If the diocesan bishop has decided to allow the celebration of the Funeral Liturgy in the presence of the cremated remains of the deceased person, care must be taken that all is carried out with due decorum. The cremated remains of the body are to be

placed in a worthy vessel. A small table or stand is to be prepared for them at the place normally occupied by the coffin. The vessel containing the cremated remains may be carried to its place in the entrance procession or may be placed on this table or stand sometime before the liturgy begins. (427)

The priest sprinkles the cremated remains with holy water, either at the door, before the entrance procession with the remains, or at the stand or table where the cremated remains were placed, after the procession. A formula is provided in OCF, U.S. Appendix 433. The paschal candle may be placed near the stand or table with the cremated remains (OCF, U.S. Appendix 435), but the placement of any kind of pall is explicitly prohibited (434). (Some well-intentioned but misguided ministers had used old chalice veils to cover the vessels holding the cremated remains. This trivializes the symbolism of the baptismal garment and funeral pall.) The altar but not the cremated remains may be honored with incense. An alternate form of dismissal is provided (437), and "[t]he Rite of Committal is celebrated at the cemetery or columbarium as soon as possible following the Funeral Liturgy." (430)

This is very new — mandated in the United States for use from November 2, 1997 — and a few preliminary observations are in order. Most funeral directors have commercially-made urns available for human ashes. It is worthwhile to contact the crematorium and ascertain whether such a vessel should be sent with the body, as some crematoria return the ashes to the family in a box or even a bag if another container is not provided. In a very large church, it may be difficult to see a small vessel with the cremated remains. Perhaps a vessel of the proper scale could be commissioned, in which smaller individual vessels could be placed for the celebration of the funeral liturgy.

Likewise, it seems better to commission a dignified stand for this vessel. The cremated remains are not to be placed on the floor, nor on the altar. Providing a stand will obviate many improvisations that might prove clumsy, such as using the credence table or a folding table borrowed from the vestibule. A stand means that the one important table, the altar, retains its prominence. And a stand whose size is appropriate to the vessel will not offer a temptation to build a shrine to the deceased with framed photos, personal mementos, flowers and plants.

Preservation and Means of Disposal of Ashes

There are further trends that seem to run counter to our Catholic value of reverent care for the remains of the human body. These include the practice of keeping the ashes or that of disposing of them by some novel means. As previously mentioned, when cremation takes place, the OCF presumes that there will be a committal of the ashes of the deceased at some time after the technological process at the crematorium, and that this committal will be an occasion of prayer. This is in keeping with the value that the church places on respect given to the corporeal remains of a human body. It is also in keeping with the Catholic community's preference for reverently burying or entombing the remains of its dead in a place reserved for the burial of the dead. There is a powerful sense of place in these burial grounds. The pastoral notes in the Canadian OCF firmly state that "liturgical rites should not accompany any method of disposal of the ashes which is not in harmony with the Christian tradition,"[11] while those in the OCF for use in England and Wales urge that "cremated remains should not normally be scattered above ground, but reverently returned to the earth."[12] It is intended that ashes be buried or entombed in a place reserved for the dead.

In the Western world there is a long history of cemeteries and places of entombment as public sacred sites. They are hallowed places, places of pilgrimage belonging to a community, where the community's dead, separated from the living, "await the glory of the resurrection" (OCF, 206). The committal of a loved one to the earth or other place of entombment is a holy event for the mourners, inaugurating for them a particular sacred site. This place is now important and holy for a number of reasons. It holds the mortal remains of our deceased sister or brother; it marks the site of separation and leave-taking; it marks the occasion when the community of faith hands the deceased over to that community which already sees God face to face. For those who hold a paschal faith, places of burial or interment speak of transformation, not preservation. They are signs that the grave, once a sign of futility and despair, is "transformed by means of Christ's own death and resurrection into a sign of hope and promise" (OCF, 209).

There is an astonishingly creative memorialization industry that promotes "attractive" ways to preserve the ashes of loved ones. These are often advertised as economical and comforting alternatives to the traditional communal resting places for the deceased. Such offers include a variety of urns (sometimes called Everlasting Urns) to be enthroned on a mantelpiece or in some place of honor in the house or family garden. If a family is uncomfortable with a repository that looks like an urn containing ashes, there are "creative" options for more discreet display — sculptured art works that may succeed in elegance but also in crass disguise. (Often in advertising, the very word "disguise" is used).

Other products of this industry include more personal means of memorialization (or privatization of death) — hand-crafted jewelry or ornaments in which the ashes of one's beloved might be encased. One sees these advertised as personal tokens by which precious memories of a loved one can be "close to you forever."

Finally, in this litany of offers from the creative memorialization industry, there are more adventurous ways of disposal of ashes: for instance, scattering ashes from a hot-air balloon at a location significant to the deceased. Such excursions are sometimes promoted as opportunities for last adventures for the deceased. These products, and others like them, are often promoted in expensive brochures as sensitive and thoughtful alternatives. Those promoting the products offer a service that leaves very little to the family in its work of completion of their care of the deceased.

There is much in this industry that is at odds with a Christian response that faces death directly. There is something very antiseptic in these trends, something that evokes yet another way that our society subtly says that death must be tamed, avoided and sanitized. Our Catholic belief is that although life is changed, not ended, death is in fact an ending. In this ending lies a hope that is not based on disappearance and transformation into another material form, in preservation in elegant art pieces, or in the hope of an adventure that eluded the deceased in life. The death of a Christian requires that the bereaved take leave, confident in a hope that is not based on cheap comfort, but on a faith that acknowledges that in the face of irretrievable loss there is the assurance that not even death can separate us from God. In death, the bereaved Christian relinquishes hold on the deceased who is handed over to God and is welcomed into the company of saints.

It is important that pastoral ministers be mindful that our Catholic faith and culture espouses reverent care of our dead:

> The remains of cremated bodies should be treated with the same respect given to the corporeal remains of a human body. This includes the manner in which they are carried, the care and attention to appropriate placement and transport, and their final disposition . . . The practices of scattering cremated remains on the sea, from the air, or on the ground or keeping cremated remains in the home of a relative or friend of the deceased are not the reverent disposition that the Church requires.[13]

A reluctance to dispose of the cremated remains of the deceased does not seem to be consistent with facing death through to its harsh end of leave-taking, of handing on to a communion beyond ourselves and our private relationships with the deceased. Nor does such reluctance give witness to a Christian understanding that in death, relationships as we have known them are ended. We have a liturgical rite that marks this ending, and which, in the midst of a community of faith, assists those who mourn to "face the end of one relationship with the deceased and begin to take up a new one based on prayerful remembrance, gratitude and the hope of resurrection and reunion" (OCF, 213). A Christian response to death does not seek hope in hanging on to the deceased, nor in the comfort of permanent reminders of the place which the deceased once held in our lives. The completion of our care for the dead asks for an act which commits the remains of our deceased to a sacred resting place. In doing this, "the community expresses a hope that, with all those who have gone before marked with the

sign of faith, the deceased awaits the glory of the resurrection."
(OCF, 206).

Given these cultural trends — offers of the "no-fuss" funerals,
immediate cremation followed by immediate disposition, and
increasingly novel forms of memorialization — our Catholic
tradition and faith must say that there is another way. It is
imperative that pastoral ministers be aware of the issues involved
in these practices. Our tradition seeks a care of the deceased
informed not by the values of the commercial marketplace, but by
a Christian hope that "faces the reality of death and the anguish
of grief, but trusts confidently that the power of sin and death has
been vanquished by the risen Lord" (OCF, 8).

CHAPTER SIX
BIRTH AND DEATH SO CLOSE TOGETHER:
FUNERAL RITES FOR CHILDREN

There Are No Answers

*Benny, just three years of age, died peacefully on a spring afternoon
after what had seemed an interminable battle with leukemia. The
day he died, his parents Ann and Peter washed his body and
lovingly dressed him in his new Raiders football outfit and laid
him on his bed. Benny's five-year-old brother, Christopher,
watched intently, every now and then patting Benny's arm.
Throughout the afternoon Christopher would disappear and then
reappear with a flower, which he would place on Benny with such
words as: "Now there's a pink one for you." As a result of these
forays into neighbors' gardens, by the end of the day, Benny was
lying in a carpet of stolen flowers. His work done, Christopher
made a place for himself among the flowers and sat beside Benny
holding his hand.*

At this point Christopher had certainly seemed to be at home
with death, although for Christmas that year he decided he didn't
want a dinosaur collection after all. He just wanted Benny back.

At the beginning of Benny's funeral, the presider, in words of
introduction, said: "I defy anyone to produce an answer that
explains Benny's death. We cannot begin to entertain the 'why' of
this death which is so much out of season and so unwelcome.
Birth and death for Benny were just three short years apart. Some

of us live in this world for a very short time and most of us much
longer. All we know today is that Benny's time with us was all too
brief, and as he lies here before us in his coffin we know that his
life has had an influence on all of us here. And we have no answers."

Much of what can be said about the experience of the death
of a child or infant can be said about any death, but in the case of
a child that experience is significantly sharpened. With the death
of a child we find ourselves standing empty-handed, nothing to
say, barraged with questions. We remember again the questioning
of C. S. Lewis as he stood empty-handed in the face of his wife
Joy's death: Did God spring a vile practical joke on even his own
Son? What kind of a God is this? Expectations, hopes and dreams
are cut short, leaving us with fragile threads and the experience
of death as a most untimely visitor, bringing overwhelming sadness
and grief, particularly for the parents and siblings. The Australian
poet James McAuley has some sense of the pain and the intensity
of the cross which marks the experience of a death so much out
of season.

> A year ago you came
> Early into the light.
> You lived a day and a night,
> Then died; no one to blame.
>
> Once only, with one hand,
> Your mother in farewell
> Touched you. I cannot tell,
> I cannot understand
>
> A thing so dark and deep,
> So physical a loss:
> One touch, and that was all

She had of you to keep.
Clean wounds, but terrible
Are those made with the Cross.[1]

So "in its pastoral ministry to the bereaved, the Christian community is challenged in a particular way by the death of an infant or a child" (OCF, 238). The Christian community cannot attempt to offer solutions; there are none. Nor can it bring an end to the pain of the parents, but can simply be companions in that pain. All that the church can offer is its presence, consolation and faith in the cross that ends not in death but in new life.

Benny, with the wisdom of a three-year-old, knew something of that faith. He had come to recognize the signs that said it was time for another visit to the hospital for more treatment. The signs were there again, but this time they were different. Benny asked his mother: "Am I going to the hospital?" "No," was the answer. "Am I going to die?" "Yes, you are going to die." "Will I close my eyes?" Again, "Yes." "And when I open them, will Olivia be there?" "Yes," replied his mother, "Olivia will be there." On Benny's visits to the hospital, he had made friends with a little girl named Olivia, but on his last visit Olivia was not there. She had died.

Throughout Benny's short life, he had been surrounded with love and tenderness. He knew the embrace of his parents, knew what it meant to be cradled in their protecting arms and knew trust in their every word and gesture. This same kind of intimacy, tenderness and trust characterizes the prayer that the church puts on the lips of the community when the death of a child summons it to gather in love and support. The funeral rites for children contained in the OCF are a beautiful body of prayer befitting the situation when a child passes in death from the arms of its parents into the loving embrace of God. Its orders of service are imbued with images of a God who at once is father, mother, author of life, one who holds and embraces, who loves tenderly, encourages intimacy and invites complete trust. And Christ, whom the bereaved experience in the presence of the community, is the compassionate Christ "who embraced little children, wept at the death of a friend, and endured the pain and separation of death in order to render it powerless over those he loves" (OCF, 239).

The Church's Action over the Body of a Deceased Child

In the OCF, an epochal shift in the funeral rites for a child who dies before baptism is seen. This action is radically different from the church's previous inaction and silence, when infants who died without baptism were buried without any liturgical ceremony. It is significant that the OCF does not use the word "unbaptized," a term which gives the sense of the unwashed, the unredeemed, but uses the phrase "children who die before baptism." The understanding is that the parents of the deceased child probably intended baptism. This welcome attitude of pastoral sensitivity should assuage any feelings of guilt or fear on the part of the parents, and eliminate any temptation toward indiscriminate or panic baptism. God has divine ways of relating to human beings in accord with divine plan. There is an assured place in the reign of God for *all* children.

The OCF does not provide separate rites for children who were baptized and those who die before baptism — children who die before baptism are no less deserving of the community's prayer. Within each of the various rites for the funeral of a child there are texts specific to each situation. Regarding the use of symbols, Christian symbols — paschal candle and cross — are used for both the baptized and the child who dies before baptism, whereas baptismal symbols — water and pall — are used only for a baptized child. In each case, the action of the community is focused differently. In the case of a baptized child, the community calls upon the riches which have been opened up in the sacrament of baptism.

For children who die before baptism, the community prayer celebrates the love of God in Jesus Christ that is the good news intended for *all*. In its prayer, the community entrusts the child to God's all-embracing love, seeking strength in this love and in Jesus' affirmation that the reign of God belongs to little children (OCF, 237).

A Ritual Process

It is not uncommon to read funeral notices for children that announce that the "Mass of the Angels" will be celebrated at a scheduled time. This is not what is offered in the OCF and pastoral ministers and funeral directors need to know this. As in the case of the death of an adult, the church, while encouraging flexibility, offers a ritual process through which the family and friends of the deceased child may find a way to express their grief and negotiate separation in a secure environment of faith. It also offers a way by which the ecclesial community can tell its story that confronts death and renders it powerless. At Benny's funeral, his mother Mary was a part of telling that story:

> *It was very important for me to be a part of Benny's funeral. When we had selected the readings, I knew that I wanted to read. Somehow, and when I look back on that day, I do not know how, I knew that I would be all right to read, and I felt that it was the last thing I could ever do for Benny. I needed to do it.*

The ritual process for children is outlined in a separate and complete section of the OCF. The process includes vigil for a deceased child, funeral Mass or funeral liturgy outside of Mass, and rite of committal. While prayers after death and gathering in the presence of the body are not included, this does not preclude surrounding these moments with prayer.

> *Midway through pregnancy, Ann-Maree and Paul were told that their child would be born severely handicapped and would die shortly after birth. Despite a certain amount of pressure from their friends, they decided to see the pregnancy through, hoping for a different outcome. Emily Maree was born after a relatively short labor. She had dark hair, very soft skin and perfectly formed little hands and feet. However, her head was incomplete and it was clear that birth and death would be very close. The parents and siblings of both Paul and Ann-Maree were present, and before leaving the hospital that night, they prayed together. Throughout the night, Ann-Maree and Paul marked each new hour with their child, especially that midnight hour, when despite all odds, Emily saw a new day. Around dawn Emily died. The family gathered again and in a prayer of commendation they entrusted Emily to the embrace of God.*

A welcome new rite in the repertoire of funeral rites for children is the rite of final commendation for an infant. It is for use in cases of stillbirth or in a case such as Emily's — an infant who dies shortly after birth. Included in this rite is a poignant blessing of the body of the deceased child. The words that the church puts on the lips of parents in this blessing are tender and sensitive: "Trusting in Jesus . . . who gathered children into his arms and blessed the little ones, we now commend this infant to that same embrace of love . . ." The blessing continues with the prayer that calls out for the touch of the infant's parents: "May the angels and saints lead him/her to the place of light and peace, where one day we will be brought together again."

As Emily lay before them, Paul and Ann-Maree were supported by this prayer of the church. The church in this very small gathering of family was with them in this time of intense grief as it prayed: "Tender Shepherd of the flock, Emily now lies cradled in your love. Soothe the hearts of her parents . . ." (OCF, 339).

An occasion such as this is bewildering and traumatic, calling for "the compassionate presence of Christ" (OCF, 239). It is not a time for busy organization, nor for a minister or chaplain to be handing out copies of an order of service. There is already a high degree of emotional intensity at this time and pastoral sensitivity demands that parents not be over-burdened. Touching the child and perhaps repeating a few phrases of the prayers after the minister might be all they can manage. This rite is necessarily brief. In its use of such images as a tender shepherd who soothes and cradles little ones, and in its expressions of needs for comfort, hope and peace, it is probably the most touching of all the rites.

Pastoral Ministry when a Child Dies

In adapting these rites, ministers are to take into account "the age of the child, the circumstances of death, the grief of the family, and the needs of those taking part in the rites" (OCF, 241). Such adaptations are not only encouraged but required. In some instances, only a rite of committal and perhaps one of the forms of prayer with the family may be desirable. Sometimes this may mean simplifying or shortening some elements of a rite and incorporating "other elements or symbols that have special meaning for those taking part in the celebration" (OCF, 246). The call is for hearing the grief of the family and ensuring that the rites and prayers proclaim a faith and a consolation that can support them in this time of tragic loss.

> *Benny loved the television character Mr. Bean, and in particular the opening segment of each of the Mr. Bean videos, when against the background music of the strains of the pipe organ, Mr. Bean hurtles down a beam of light, and whoosh, lands bemused on the pavement. Benny often asked for this part of the video to be played when he was too sick to do anything else. The homilist at Benny's funeral began by playing the soundtrack of this Mr. Bean segment. Those who had been close to Benny knew that Benny loved the music. It must have soothed him. They also knew Benny's infectious giggle that bubbled up every time he watched the video. It was laughter that taught them so much about the ordinariness of life, of suffering in the midst of the ordinary and of the extraordinary influence and witness of a little child.*

Of course, the very mention of Mr. Bean called up memories of Benny. Since this Mr. Bean segment had brought such joy to Benny and to the family, its inclusion in the homily was naturally at home.

It was actually through the incorporation of this element that the homilist ingeniously opened up the mystery of suffering and death that took place in the midst of life. He invited those present to reflect on how God had worked in the life and death of Jesus and in the life and death of Benny and continues to work in our lives. While in the face of Benny's death, the community had no explanations, Benny's life had meaning, and the ordinariness and the influence of his life and death was what remained. This homily was indeed a wonderful marrying of life and faith.

It is important to remember that even in the case of the death of a child, the church's ministry of consolation and prayer is primarily for those who suffer the pain of loss. The funeral of a deceased child usually involves intense parental grief, and part of the ministry of the church at this time is to ensure the articulation of a hope that can support adult faith. This is not to say that the OCF is inattentive to the needs of children who may be present at the funeral. On the contrary, it encourages the presence and involvement of children, as well as adaptations made in the interests of the faith of childhood. This is a delicate matter, with implications for selections of music, prayers and readings. Somehow, the liturgy must speak hopefully to both adults and children. But the funeral of a deceased child cannot remain at the level of "cute." To celebrate the funeral of a child in terms relevant only to children would do serious disservice in a situation of intense parental grief.

At the death of a child, the Christian community is greatly challenged in its pastoral ministry. The church's care on such occasions must draw on the gifts and experience of many. "Those who have lost children of their own may be able in a special way to help the family as they struggle to accept the death of a child" (OCF, 240). Parents will always remember their experience of church at such a time. A constant reminder in the pastoral notes that accompany the funeral rites for children in the OCF is the need for awareness, understanding and sensitivity on the part of all who minister. We have a very touching body of prayer in the rites, informed by a sound psychology and spirituality of grief. They constitute a structured and yet very flexible ritual process upon which to draw with sensitivity, faithfulness and creativity, a ritual through which the ecclesial community can truly exercise its ministry of care and consolation.

PART III

WORK AROUND AND BEYOND THE RITES

CHAPTER SEVEN
THE PARISH FUNERAL AND SUNDAY EUCHARIST

CHAPTER SEVEN
The Parish Funeral and Sunday Eucharist

We Come Here Sunday after Sunday

The parish community of what had once been a large mining town had been told that soon they would be without a resident priest. Fortunately, the diocese had in place a process to form parish leaders and to prepare the community for this significant change. At the conclusion of a formation session for funeral ministers, one member of the group asked why we went to all this trouble of having the funeral at church; he thought it might be simpler if the funeral took place at the funeral home. The priest's response was simple: "Because we come here Sunday after Sunday." He continued: "This is the place where we baptize, we confirm, we marry, we come for healing. So this is the place, our place, from which we bid farewell and bury."

The assumption of the OCF is that the ritual environment of the Christian funeral is the parish liturgical assembly, the strongest expression of which is the Sunday eucharistic action of the community. This is not to say that the funerals of deceased members of a community must necessarily take place on Sunday, but rather that there is a strong and intimate connection between the funeral of a Christian and the Sunday eucharistic assembly. Whether or not the deceased had been an active member of that Sunday gathering is not the question. Rather, because the deceased was baptized, he or she had an ecclesial identity, which in turn meant a rightful place in that assembly whenever it gathered. If this relationship is not understood, it makes little sense for the funeral of a Christian to take place within the context of a parish liturgical assembly.

Sunday after Sunday, week by week, year by year, worshipers, regardless of numbers, come to celebrate the eucharist, the action that marks them as a community of the baptized, which lives out of the life, death and resurrection of Jesus. Sunday after Sunday, this gathering brings to its worship its own daily deaths and resurrections and opens itself to the transforming power of the death and resurrection of Jesus. In doing so, this gathering engages in a meaningful act of word and sacrament, the act by which members recommit themselves to the terms of their baptism and to lives congruent with their identity in Christ. It is this eucharistic act of the Sunday liturgical assembly that gives highest expression to the paschal mystery, the mystery of death and resurrection within which and out of which the Christian lives. What more fitting ritual environment for a believing community to mark the death of one of its members?

At the death of a Christian, this same liturgical assembly is called to a ministry that flows from its baptismal identity:

> [T]hose who are baptized into Christ and nourished at the same table are responsible for one another. . . . So too when a member of Christ's Body dies, the faithful are called to a ministry of consolation. . . . The Church calls each member of Christ's Body . . . to participate in the ministry of consolation. (OCF, 8)

Thus "the responsibility for the ministry of consolation rests with the believing community" (OCF, 9). While the community expresses this ministry in different ways through the grieving time of those who mourn, it is brought to special focus in the liturgy. This is a responsibility that derives from baptism and from the Lord's command to "do this in memory of me."

Sunday by Sunday, members of the liturgical assembly learn of their responsibility to one another and that "if one member suffers in the body of Christ which is the church, all the members suffer with that member" (1 CORINTHIANS 12:26). Sunday by Sunday the "gathered community for worship . . . announces and brings to fuller expression [its] affinity with Christ's own dying and rising."[1] At the death of one of its members, the believing community gathers to give thanks for and give baptismal farewell to one of its own, and in a memorial act celebrates a paschal faith that proclaims that death is broken by the transforming power of the death and resurrection of Jesus. The death of Jesus is indeed the prototype of all our deaths.

We do "come here Sunday after Sunday," and much of what we do at our Sunday gatherings we do at funerals. In fact, we know what to do at funerals and how to do it because of what we do in the Sunday liturgical assembly. At that weekly gathering we assemble because it matters. We welcome and receive new Christians, we proclaim, listen to, respond to, preach and break open God's word. We intercede, give thanks and bless, we offer ourselves, make a gesture of peace, eat and drink food for the life of the world, commit ourselves to the life and mission of Jesus. We sing, we acclaim, we stand and sit, we make the sign of the cross, we keep prayerful silence. We engage in symbolic activity and ritual dialogue. And the grace and dignity with which we do all these things Sunday by Sunday will be the measure of a parish's funeral practice.

Since much of what we do at the Christian funeral is baptismal, it stands to reason that our funeral practice will be as grace-filled as our baptismal practice. If initiation truly takes place within the context of a robust ecclesial environment of faith and in the midst of that community's liturgical assembly, then a community comes to expect that it must give farewell to one of its members in that same context. The cluster of symbols used at baptism — water, candle, white garment, cross, word, bread and wine, and a community of faith — are the same cluster that surround death. If there is a lavishness and care in our use of these symbols at the annual Easter Vigil and the weekly Sunday celebrations, then those baptismal aspects of our funeral rites will have far more chance of speaking of a journey of faith begun in the waters of baptism which in death is not ended, but transformed.

It is imperative that pastoral ministers in our parishes understand that our funeral rites do not stand alone and apart from our Sunday eucharistic assemblies, nor indeed from the Great Sunday celebration of the Easter Vigil. Unless there is a regular Sunday practice that is mindful, gracious and in touch with the daily deaths and resurrections of people's lives, then there will be little foundation for a funeral practice that embodies all that it means to live and die as a Christian.

The Music of Our Sunday and Funeral Assemblies[2]

Amanda buried her mother the day before her marriage to Michael. Her mother had died suddenly and the decision was made to continue with the wedding plans as arranged. Amanda had no siblings, her father was dead and she had only a few relatives; it was expected that the funeral be small. There would be a funeral Mass followed by a graveside committal. The funeral took place in her mother's parish church, which was huge, cavernous and cold. The day was extremely bleak and wintry, which did not help the occasion. The first sound heard at the funeral Mass was the organ, exquisitely played, but exuberant and triumphant. The sound carried an expectation that this small and very fragile group of mourners would launch into full-bodied song: "In faith and hope and love/with joyful trust we move/toward our Father's home above." Meanwhile Amanda and Michael self-consciously walked down the center aisle to take their seats.

On this occasion, the strong words of hope and joyful trust (to say nothing of the organ's sound) seemed not to fit; they asked too much too soon. Given the combination of events and circumstances surrounding the death of Amanda's mother, this funeral shuddered with numbness and bewilderment, confusion and deep sadness. It cried out for music of lament, for music that could both embrace and unveil grief, for a sound that was deeply sensitive to the peculiarity and intense pain of the occasion. The circumstances that surrounded this sudden death (and indeed every death) demanded that the "music for the celebration . . . be chosen with great care" (OCF, 31). The lack of fit on this occasion suggests that there was little care taken in the choice of music, that there was little sensitivity to the needs of Amanda and her family at this traumatic time. The music was in fact alienating and served to mask feelings and emotions. It is possible that the music used for this funeral was used for all funerals in this parish, regardless of the circumstances of death.

Since music has so significant a role in life in general, it is only natural that we seek to ritualize with music any significant event in our lives, especially a reality as significant as death. The document *Music in Catholic Worship* speaks of the power of music to "unveil a dimension of meaning and feeling . . . which words alone cannot yield" (MCW, 24). About the power of music in the midst of death, one author writes: "Singing is discovered and invented; it is born at times when there is no other possible way for people to express themselves — at the grave . . . where four or five people with untrained, clumsy voices sing words that are greater and smaller than their faith and their experience."[3]

Understandably, in marking the death of a Christian with liturgical rites, the church has always turned to music to help give expression to our experience of the unfathomable mystery of death and life through death. The OCF acknowledges the potential and power of music, making it a constitutive liturgical element in our funeral rites:

> Music is integral to the funeral rites. It allows the community to express convictions and feeling that words alone may fail to convey. It has the power to console and uplift the mourners and to strengthen the unity of the assembly in faith and love. (OCF, 30)

The OCF does not take up questions of repertoire and musical style. It merely gives a broad directive that there be music at the vigil, the funeral liturgy and when possible at the funeral processions and the rite of committal. The rite specifies that music be chosen that is consonant with and expressive of the Christian attitude to death: "The texts of the songs chosen for a particular celebration should express the paschal mystery of the Lord's suffering, death and triumph over death . . ." (OCF, 30).

When we look at the rites of the OCF as a whole, there is a thematic unity throughout. Over and over again the life-death-life motif weaves through the rites, assuring mourners that "life is changed, not ended," and that Christ who has conquered death has gone before us, flinging open "the gates of life," the "gates of paradise" — all in readiness to welcome home the one who has died.

In the case of the funeral of Amanda's mother, the opening song certainly spoke of a life-death-life passage. Its text did indeed express the paschal mystery, articulating a fitting Christian response of hope and thanksgiving. However, while meeting a liturgical and theological requirement, one might well pose a question at the pastoral level: Was it appropriate for this occasion and for these particular people and their needs at this time? The musical sound this moment called for was not Easter exuberance, but a sound that was restrained, consonant with and sensitive to the confused and deep feelings of the occasion, and at the same time faith-filled.

Rose's funeral, where the music had been thoughtfully considered, was very different.

Rose was of Irish heritage. Throughout her life she had delighted many with her gift of song. She had sung at the weddings of many who now gathered for her funeral, and at the funerals of many who had gone before her. Rose's funeral Mass concluded with the words, "Rose, your voice is silent now. May the song of the angels welcome you and guide you along the way of this last journey. Let us now take Rose to her place of rest." Rose's grandchildren proudly and tenderly carried her from the church to the nearby grave,

*accompanied by an Irish jig played on a tin whistle. As people
gathered around Rose's grave, there were tears, there was hope,
there was joy. And of course there was deep sorrow.*

On this occasion, the wordless Irish jig was not the sound of Easter
exuberance, but somehow it was the right sound, a fitting way to
pipe this woman of song into the company of the angels.

Sensitivity, care and appropriateness should dominate our
thinking when choosing music for the Christian funeral. If music
is to be appropriate, it must be so at every level, not just at the
level of theology. We need to hold in balance musical, liturgical and
pastoral considerations when choosing music for our worship. In
the case of the funeral of Amanda's mother, the level of pastoral
sensitivity seemed to have been unattended to.

Mindful of the paschal "life-death-life" motif that forms the
bedrock of the Christian funeral, it is useful to attend again to the
ritual process of the OCF in which each rite has its own place,
intent, mood and meaning. It may be helpful to consider the public
rites of the OCF as a three-movement concerto or symphony, in
which each movement — each rite — has its own tempo, mood,
sound and character.

What music is appropriate to the vigil (first movement) with
its mood of quiet, stillness, waiting, dwelling with death? What
music, what sound, what sentiments are appropriate to the funeral
liturgy (second movement) with its baptismal themes, dying with
Christ, rising to new life, themes of thanksgiving, farewell and
commendation? In the rite of committal (third movement)
mourners are asked to take leave, to commit their loved one to the
earth or fire, to God. With its strong images of "earth to earth,"
"ashes to ashes," "dust to dust," as well as "communion of saints"

and "eternal rest," what music, what strains of sound (or perhaps of silence) will assist mourners in this "stark and powerful expression of separation" (OCF, 213)? There is a completeness about each movement of the symphony, and yet the music of the symphony is the music of the whole. There is an appropriate music for each of the rites, and the music of the funeral is the music of the whole. Throughout the symphonic movement of these rites, pastoral ministers and musicians need to ensure that the music "support, console, and uplift the participants and . . . help to create in them a spirit of hope in Christ's victory over death and in the Christian's share in that victory" (OCF, 31).

There is always concern about the potential and capacity for singing at funerals. Some argue that it is too difficult a time to expect people to sing, that our funeral assemblies are too diverse, that funerals are not the occasion to teach new songs. Some parishes have overcome the difficulty by forming small parish funeral choirs. Members of the parish with flexible schedules, perhaps those who are retired, are often willing to be part of this ministry of supporting the assembly in its prayer and song. Some organization is necessary so that its song will indeed be ministerial and provide the care and consolation called for by the occasion of death.

The question of repertoire need not be a difficult one for a parish, particularly if there is already an organized music ministry that begins with the Sunday assembly. If a parish has a singing assembly on Sunday then there is no reason why it will not have a singing assembly at the funeral for one of its members. If a parish has a well-thought-out Sunday repertoire that carries the parish through the liturgical year, there is already an assured repertoire for funerals. There are times in the liturgical year that may be borrowed from to strengthen such a repertoire.

1. A good start is with the second memorial acclamation: "Dying you destroyed our death, rising you restored our life. Lord Jesus, come in glory." The setting the parish uses throughout November might serve. A parish could have two settings, one that is restrained in mood and another that has an Easter feel to it.

2. Lent-Easter: Strong death-resurrection hymns and acclamations can be introduced during these seasons.

3. Ordinary Time: The last Sundays of each liturgical year all deal with eschatological events and the second coming of Christ in glory. If the parish already knows a selection of hymns and acclamations appropriate to these Sundays, then it can draw on these for its funerals.

4. November: This might be a good time to sing again the Litany of the Saints sung at the Easter Vigil. A setting of this litany can be very appropriate for funerals. If a parish has an annual celebration for all who have died over the year, this is yet another occasion to use music that can be part of a funeral repertoire.

5. Psalms: Throughout the three-year cycle, it seems important that a parish has a repertoire of psalms such as: Psalm 23 (The Lord is my shepherd); Psalm 26 (The Lord is my light and my help); Psalm 102 (The Lord is compassion and love); Psalm 129 (Out of the depths I cry to you, O Lord).

In addition to the parish "year-round" repertoire, a parish does need to have a small repertoire specific to funerals. Songs that speak of the immediacy of death, of raw grief, as well as songs of farewell, come to mind. Mention has already been made of the need for a song of farewell which is suitable for the final commendation and farewell. It would not be difficult to introduce one setting of "Saints of God" in which the assembly sings the refrain:

"Receive her/his soul and present her/him to God the Most High." This, in time, might become the song with which every member of the parish is bid farewell. Music specifically for the funeral of a Christian is becoming more and more accessible.[4] In addition to special collections, music for various parts of the rites can be found in the service sections of most recently published hymnals and service music collections.[5]

In planning a funeral repertoire, well-known, familiar tunes are essential to ensuring that people will sing. It is easy to say that if we have singing Sunday assemblies, then we will have singing funeral assemblies. But the funeral assembly is a unique and diverse gathering involving some members of the Sunday assembly and often a conglomerate of people who may or may not have ever been together before and who probably will never come together again. People of all faiths and no faith come to funerals, just as do people who have regular or varying degrees of association with church. Pastoral musicians need to keep this in mind. It is all the more reason that a funeral repertoire include not only music from the Sunday assembly, but also familiar tunes and some old favorites. "Amazing Grace" and "How Great Thou Art" come to mind. Contemporary texts set to traditional melodies are very useful for this purpose.[6]

A pastoral issue arises when requests are made for songs that do not fall into the category of "sacred," or do not express "the paschal mystery of the Lord's suffering, death and triumph over death" (ocf, 30). The local football song certainly does not fit this category. This situation must always be sensitively handled. On the one hand, this is not the time to be teaching the bereaved what is appropriate and what is not; on the other hand, the community of faith reserves the right to proclaim its faith that death does not have the last word. There is no easy solution to this question. Pastoral ministers cannot afford to offend the bereaved, and must always be ready to dialogue. The situation highlights several needs: the need for sound catechesis on our funeral rites and on the nature of liturgy itself; the need for attentive ministers who can deal with such situations with discretion and sensitivity; the need for good modeling of funeral celebrations so that people come to know what they can expect of the church at the funeral of a Christian. It would be very helpful if parish funeral ministry teams were to draw up guidelines for the celebration of funerals including suggestions for music appropriate for the Christian funeral.

The question of recorded music is worthy of attention. The merits of recorded music are to be weighed against "the long-term impact . . . on the local assembly and their common worship."[7] The argument for "live" participation, according to the U.S. Bishops' Committee on the Liturgy, lies in the fact that "the liturgy is a complexus of signs experienced by living human beings. Music, being pre-eminent among these signs, ought to be 'live'".[8] From a different perspective—an analysis of the media presence in our lives—what has been said of the media can be applied to recorded music: "As a pervasive and persuasive presence in our midst the media can do much to enhance our lives."[9] The same writer continues: "It can also become so dominant a presence that we may risk losing our proper independence of thought and action."[10] This is the point in the consideration of recorded music in our common worship. There are times when resources are so slim that well-selected recorded music can truly enhance our funeral celebrations, and in fact support the ritual engagement of the assembly. A problem arises when a parish relies solely on recorded music in the continuing belief that "live" music is not possible.

Questions to be asked in discussing the issue of participation and recorded music are "first and foremost whether the recording will enable or impede the community's participation,"[11] and whether the short-term advantages achieved through its use will impede the long-term outcome.

The role of music in funeral ministry is not to be underestimated. If indeed it is to fulfill its function in our funeral liturgies, allowing the community "to express convictions and feelings that words alone may fail to convey" (OCF, 50), it must be faith-filled and at the same time capture a language of death that is bold, fearless and true. In the face of death, the Christian cannot be content with the sweet and saccharine that often tries to mask the reality of death. The Christian in faith and in song must name things as they are: grief, longing, trust, reality and a sure hope grounded in the death and resurrection of Jesus.

Year-Round Remembrance of the Dead

The grieving, the sense of loss, the loneliness that are the legacy of the death of a loved one do not come to an end with the committal of the deceased to his or her final place of rest. It is often in the weeks and months after the intense days of the funeral that grief and the sense of loss are at their most intense. So too the community's ministry of consolation begun in the funeral rites does not come to its completion when the deceased is laid to rest. In fact, it is the community's presence and prayer throughout the funeral rites that "signifies their intention to support the mourners in the time following the funeral" (OCF, 213) as the bereaved continue their work of taking up a new relationship with the deceased.

The ministry of consolation calls for attentive pastoral care of the bereaved beyond the time of the funeral. For the wider community of faith, this care for the bereaved takes shape in prayerful remembrance as it gathers year-round for worship. Week by week, there is opportunity for this remembrance in the prayers of intercession of the Sunday liturgical assembly. In a final intention, the recently deceased are named and held in loving memory, as well as those deceased members of the community whose anniversaries fall around the same time. It is easy for this final intercession to get lost in a perfunctory recitation of a weekly formula. Those responsible for preparing Sunday liturgy need to be thoughtful in formulating the intercession for the deceased. One formula might be: "In a moment of silence, let us remember N. who died during this week (and whose name has been inscribed in our Book of the Dead) . . . (silence) . . . We remember too all of our deceased, especially those whose anniversaries occur at this time of the year, (names)." Much depends on the silence that surrounds the naming of the recently deceased and the manner in which the litany of anniversaries is read. This is an opportunity for communal remembering so that the community might continue its work of consolation and prayer. A minister who reads this intercession like a list of names from a telephone book or who, through lack of preparation, stumbles over pronunciation of names, will not succeed in leading the community in a remembrance that is prayerful and consoling to those close to the deceased.

The anniversary of death is yet another occasion for remembering the deceased and the bereaved, and an opportunity for a parish to exercise its ministry of pastoral care beyond the rites. Besides naming the deceased in the prayers of intercession around the anniversary, a parish might offer the ministry of specific household prayer for the first anniversary. The pastoral care or bereavement team might prepare a small booklet of resources for such an occasion, basing it on prayers and orders of service already in the OCF and supplementary sources.[12] A simple format could include a greeting, prayer, scripture reading, prayers of intercession, the Lord's Prayer and a blessing. Close to the time of the anniversary, a pastoral minister might visit the family to prepare for the prayer and then also be present at the time of the prayer. This presumes an organized ministry of care in the parish so that anniversaries can be anticipated and so that ministers are available to prepare and lead prayer with the family or household.

A number of parishes have their own Book of the Names of the Dead in which the names of the deceased are inscribed. Throughout the year, this book could reside in a place of honor somewhere near the baptismal font and paschal candle. During the month of November, it might be solemnly placed in a prominent position. At the prayers of intercession during the liturgies of the month, it could be held aloft as the community prays in remembrance of all whose names are inscribed in it.

November has traditionally been the month for remembering the deceased, a month that begins with the celebrations of All Saints and All Souls (Commemoration of All the Faithful Departed). Writing about the celebration of the Day of the Dead in Mexico, Gabrielle Carey reflects on her own experience of this celebration:

> The Day of the Dead became an important tradition to me in Mexico simply because it filled a need I had felt so badly for so long: the need to have time to reflect on the death of lost friends and relatives. . . . For a few days, the Day of the Dead allowed the shadows of my dead friends and relatives to come into relief, to be recognized and respected for the love and grief

they still inspire, that still endures. . . . The Day of the Dead allows a person to come closer to the siren without having to be fatally seduced. It is almost like familiarizing yourself with your ultimate enemy, an enemy you know it is impossible to defeat and to whom you will one day have to surrender.[13]

This experience speaks of the value and the importance of a time during the year when societies can collectively and personally remember their dead. For the church this time is November, the month of the dead, and perhaps there is much to be retrieved in our November practices. As noted above, the Book of the Names of the Dead could be given more prominence during this month. At each of the Sunday liturgies, Eucharistic Prayer IV with its specific remembrance of the deceased might be prayed: "Remember those who have died in the peace of Christ and all the dead whose faith is known to you alone." November also lends itself to special celebrations for all those who have died during the year; often, this will be a Memorial Mass. It does not seem sufficient to promote these Masses in the parish bulletin as if it were the parish festival. The gesture of a written invitation to the families of the bereaved is far more personal, a gesture that says that they and their loved ones have not been forgotten. At these liturgies, there could be a procession with the Book of the Names of the Dead accompanied by a solemn proclamation of names.

November is also a good opportunity for a parish to introduce and pray Morning or Evening Prayer from the Office for the Dead. This could be scheduled once a week, providing an opportunity for a parish to pray its way through the month and in psalms of lament and thanksgiving to hold the deceased of the parish in loving memory. The parish Book of the Names of the Dead could be part of each celebration. Few parishes are familiar with this prayer. If a parish is to begin to pray it during November, its format needs to be simple and repetitive, incorporating the use of the paschal candle and baptismal water. To assist in this praying, the Sunday parish bulletin might include each week some simple catechesis on some aspect of the prayer: prayer at morning and evening; the shape of morning and evening prayer; the psalms — the core of the prayer; the psalms — cries of the human heart.

It might also be possible during this month for a parish to arrange for a pilgrimage to the cemetery in the vicinity. Families could certainly be encouraged to visit the graves of their loved ones during this month of remembering. Simple family prayer leaflets could be prepared for these visits.[14]

These are ways by which the deceased are assured a place in the collective memory of the parish. They are opportunities for "the shadows of . . . dead friends and relatives to come into relief, to be recognized and respected for the love and grief they still inspire, that still endures."[15] They are moments in which we the living, still to face our own deaths, can familiarize ourselves with death, so that death when it comes will not be the enemy of which Carey speaks, but rather may be a friend, or in the words of Francis of Assisi, even a sister. They are opportunities for the believing community to continue to remember its responsibility for pastoral care at the time of death and beyond. Occasions for prayer in the midst of a community of faith can assist those close to the bereaved to remember that the bonds forged in life are not broken, and that the bonds in death are built on "prayerful remembrance, gratitude, and the hope of resurrection and reunion" (OCF, 213).

Catechesis toward a New Practice

There are parishes still today that are not aware that the church has a very particular form of ritual prayer to be used when it gathers to mark the death of one of its members. It is not rare to find priests with attitudes such as: "A funeral is a funeral is a funeral," or "I've been doing funerals for years and I'm not going to change now." With this being so, it is little wonder that the riches of the *Order of Christian Funerals* remain foreign territory to some parishes. It follows that if the overall liturgical life of a parish is not taken with a degree of thoughtfulness and seriousness, the implementation of renewed rites such as the OCF will be given little attention.

In chapter three, the story was told of a funeral during which one of the community asked: "Is this kind of thing done only for nuns?" The story was also told in which Brad, not knowing any other way, asked if the priest could come to anoint his wife who had just died. Incidents like this point to the need for catechesis. How does a parish move into new ways of doing things in keeping with the vision of new rites?

Attention needs to be given to the role of local bishops as first teachers in their dioceses, catechesis and formation of our ritual leaders and catechesis of the parish community. While the concern of this book is mainly parish catechesis, let us not forget that it is incumbent on bishops as first teachers of the liturgy and on priests as pastoral leaders of parish communities to be active in their own catechesis and formation. It is often presumed that our ordained leaders are exempt from steeping themselves in the vision of new rites, and that it is "the people" who are the ones in need of formation. Not so! All who lead the prayer of our new rites for funerals need to do some necessary homework. Questions to be asked might include: What is renewed in the OCF? Can we simply look at these new rites as if they are the same as the old, but with new names? What is the significance of the title of this new book? What do these rites ask of a presider that was not asked in our previous rites? What kind of ministry, preparation and participation does this Order ask for? Given that the nature of the OCF as a ritual book is not a simple, ready-made ritual in which all is laid out in every detail for every circumstance, how might we make it manageable? What are the implications of this new Order for current praxis? What needs to be done if the whole parish is to claim these rites as its own?

Well-prepared celebration of the church's ritual prayer always does a significant amount of catechesis, but it is unjust to expect the rites to carry the full burden. Experience of the rites done well needs to be accompanied by intentional catechesis. While pastoral ministers might undertake this in a more in-depth forum, it seems that the best time for catechesis of the wider parish is when the community is gathered for Sunday eucharist. Such an approach might be planned in conjunction with the Sunday lectionary. It does demand thoughtful planning ahead of time. It should also be done alongside other forms of sacramental catechesis.

A time that lends itself readily to catechesis on the OCF is the last Sundays of the liturgical year when the lectionary readings have a distinctly eschatological focus. The fact that these Sundays occur in November is a further reason for the appropriateness of this time. Planners would need to select particular aspects of the OCF to which to give attention. A schema might include the responsibility of the community of faith in time of sickness and death; death and the Christian response to death; the funeral process embodied in the OCF; the symbols of baptism — the symbols at death; household prayer at the time of death. The method for this catechesis could take the form of preaching on each of the above aspects, supplemented by relevant bulletin inserts or take-home sheets. Questions that people often ask could be addressed in these sheets: Can the dead be anointed? Where does the rosary fit? What does the church do when children die? Can Catholics be cremated?

There is no way that this catechesis can be complete in a single year, but it is crucial that the community of faith not be left with no catechesis at all. Formal catechesis has its place, as does the experience of the liturgical assembly at the time of death. With household prayer at the time of death and anniversaries, inclusion of the deceased in our Sunday prayer, prayer for the deceased during November — all of this together can constitute a catechesis that puts before believers their responsibility for pastoral care in the time of death, a care that takes its form in mutual charity and comfort and in active participation in the celebration of the funeral rites.

An Organized Ministry of Pastoral and Ritual Care

Throughout this book reference has frequently been made to "an organized ministry." If the ministry of pastoral and ritual care envisioned in the OCF is to be brought about, it must be organized and implemented. Most frequently, death comes after a time of sickness and a period of dying. For this reason the ministry of consolation of which the OCF speaks does not stand alone, but continues the care that already takes place in situations of sickness and dying. Throughout the time of sickness, dying, death and bereavement, the church is called to a ministry of pastoral care that takes shape in a real and active presence of comfort, consolation and prayer.

When Christians are sick, their brothers and sisters share a ministry of mutual charity and do all that they can to help the sick return to health by showing love for the sick and by celebrating the sacraments with them. So too when a member of Christ's body dies, the faithful are called to a ministry of consolation to those who have suffered the loss of one whom they love (OCF, 8).

The ritual care outlined in the OCF continues the ritual process of *Pastoral Care of the Sick: Rites of Anointing and Viaticum* (PCS).

Just as death does not happen in a vacuum, neither does the ministry of the church at the time of death exist in a vacuum. That ministry cannot simply happen because a death has happened. The ministry envisioned by both PCS and the OCF presumes a community of faith that recognizes its responsibility for care, and knows that its ministry in times of sickness and death must be mindfully and intentionally ensured. It presumes a community whose presence is palpable through active care, not just at the hour of death, but throughout the whole time of sickness and dying. A parish that already cares for its sick and for its dying is the parish that best cares for the deceased and for the bereaved who face taking leave of one whom they have loved. Because of our baptismal identity and commitment, such ministry cannot be the sole preserve of the ordained ministers of the church. This ministry demands the serious attention of all in various degrees. There is no place for a haphazard approach.

The following is the endeavor of one parish — large, multi-cultural and urban — to set in place an organized ministry that ensures, as far as possible, the presence of the church throughout the critical times of dying, death and bereavement.

The coordinator of the parish pastoral life team records:

It was not actually the publication of the Order of Christian
Funerals *that inspired the funeral ministry in our parish, although
I believe we had been using it from the time it was approved for
use. Eight years ago, after a parish assembly, the pastoral team
made the decision to employ a half-time liturgy coordinator in the
parish, and that decision proved to be key in the development of
our overall liturgical life. It was very clear that the people of our
parish had come to have expectations of the Sunday liturgy, and
that was where we decided to put our efforts. A liturgy committee
was formed, ministry training programs were put in place and a
lot of effort was put into our ministry of music. Preaching was also
given a high priority. As our Sunday worship became more
participative and life-giving, people seemed to become more
involved in other aspects of parish life, particularly outreach. We
felt that we were taking much more responsibility for the life of the
parish, not just leaving this to the priests. Somewhere in all of this
were the beginnings of our funeral ministry. I suppose we began to
see other possibilities beyond our Sunday worship.*

*The other factor in the development of our funeral ministry
arose out of the practical situation of ministry with the varied
ethnic communities of the parish. We perceived that there was a
"pastoral gap" when people of different ethnic backgrounds died,
and felt that for effective ministry, their own people needed to be
involved. Initially, involvement was quite informal, often at the
level of translation. This in time led to further involvement.*

*Our more formal ministry began with three Sundays of
preaching on ministry at the time of both sickness and death, our
intention being to form a small funeral ministry team. On the*

third of these Sundays, the homilist spoke of how this team might be involved. We invited two people whom we felt would have a natural gift for this ministry to be part of the team, but at the same time extended the invitation to the whole parish. We formed a small team of five, and over a period of a year, did a lot of in-servicing, sometimes taking advantage of opportunities offered by the diocese, at others organizing our own study sessions of the OCF. Over this time, when a member of the parish died, one member of the team would accompany the priest on the occasion of the first pastoral visit to the family and would subsequently be involved in the preparation of the liturgy, and in some cases lead some part of the liturgy.

There was much discussion at the time regarding the scheduling of funerals, and out of this came another significant decision. The responsibility of the whole community at the time of death had been an aspect of the Sunday preaching. Our pastoral life and funeral ministry teams agreed that the best way by which the community could be with the bereaved at the time of death would be to schedule funerals, as far as possible, at the weekday Mass time. While there are sometimes problems with this, particularly when we have a run of funerals, this decision has certainly heightened parish awareness of ministry at the time of death and assures the presence of some members of the Sunday community.

As time has gone on and as confidence has grown, the funeral ministry team has taken on more responsibility. When the priest is notified of a death, he usually makes the initial pastoral visit to the family, and depending on circumstances, suggests that one of the parish funeral ministry team visit at another time to help prepare the funeral liturgy. To help with this preparation, we have prepared our own book which contains the readings from the OCF and a few others which we have added, some models of prayers of intercession, and a collection of hymns — opening songs, communion and recessional songs. Because we ourselves have grown in our understanding of the OCF, we are actually at a stage of revising the hymn section to include grieving songs and songs of farewell. Usually we will leave this book with the family; it functions as a kind of parish handbook for funerals. Often, families will have special requests, particularly for music, and we always try to see where these will best fit. When the liturgy has been prepared, we offer the services of the parish secretary for the printing of an order of service, and we have found that the simpler this is, the better, particularly for very mixed congregations. It's important that people know when to sit and stand, and that they have the texts of the songs. The funeral minister is the one who then dialogues with the presider for the funeral liturgy, the organist and the coordinator of the funeral ministry team.

If there is to be a vigil or a rosary, the funeral minister usually leads it. On the day of the funeral, the funeral minister is present to meet the family, to rehearse those who will have a particular part in the service — so that they will feel comfortable — and to ensure that the very practical things are attended to. The funeral minister is usually part of the entrance procession, leads the rite of reception and then leads part of the graveside or crematorium service.

Alongside the funeral ministry team, we now have a bereavement group as well as a team of people who are always willing to help with preparation of food. A number of people in the parish who wanted to be involved in ministry at the time of death felt that the liturgy was not their thing and that they could contribute in other ways. This is how the bereavement group was formed and it is coordinated by a member of the parish who is a palliative care nurse at a local hospice. Often, members of this group are involved in pastoral care after the time of the funeral. They visit the bereaved families, often a month after the death. One of the members ensures that each family receives a card on the anniversary of death and that each is involved in household prayer on the anniversary occasion. This group is also very involved in the organization of parish memorial Masses which we have twice a year.

As this ministry has grown, we have found that it is essential that there be a key person to keep his or her finger on the pulse and that there always be collaboration with the priests of the parish. We meet as a team about four or five times a year, and on these occasions we reflect together on our experiences, pray, share new resources and take opportunities for further formation. Ministry at the time of death is a very rewarding one, but it is also very demanding, and so we value these meetings and the mutual support which we experience through them. As funeral ministers, we feel that we are a very real part of the pastoral care which is called for at the time of death. The parish has come to accept us and to expect our involvement, and often people will request a particular minister to help in the preparation of the liturgy. We don't feel that we are there simply "to help Father," or because "Father is too busy." This is real ministry for us, and we take our responsibility very seriously.

The *Ministry* of the Church and the *Service* of the Funeral Directors

Who offers what at the death of a Christian? The OCF is very clear that when a Christian dies, the church, the believing community, offers a ministry to the mourners and to the deceased and that such ministry finds its source in the event of baptism: "Those who are baptized into Christ and nourished at the same table of the Lord are responsible for one another" (OCF, 8). The believing community is the body of Christ that when "one member suffers in the body . . . all the members suffer with that member" (OCF, 8). It is because of this oneness in Christ, and of the deceased's life in Christ, that the responsibility for consolation cannot be an option for the community of faith. It is the church's responsibility to comfort and console the mourners and to be with them in prayer as they mourn for their loved one and as they complete their care for the deceased. Throughout this ministry the church professes its belief in the paschal mystery and announces that in death, while life as we know it is ended, the deceased now enjoys a life that has defeated death, a life that continues beyond the grave. This is the thrust of the church's ministry at the death of a Christian.

The service of the funeral director does not necessarily find its source in baptism, nor in oneness in the body of Christ. The funeral industry is involved in the business of assisting mourners in all that needs to be done, in order that the body of the deceased be laid to rest in a manner that is respectful and dignified. Their primary service, although this is by no means the only one, lies in the preparation and transfer of the body of the deceased. This work of the funeral profession is very focused and clearly very different from the work that is rightly the church's in the face of death.

In recent years the services of the funeral industry have expanded greatly. Many funeral homes now offer the service of grief counseling. As an alternative to the traditional church building, many offer the use of a comfortable funeral home chapel where the bereaved might bid farewell to the one they have loved; this often attracts those who have little or no association with the institutional church. Along with this there is often the provision of the minister to lead the memorial or farewell service. Some funeral homes have also designed their own orders of service. As previously mentioned, as cremation becomes a more preferred means of disposition, some funeral homes provide alternatives to traditional means of disposition of ashes — creative memorialization.

This is not to suggest that funeral directors do not have the right to offer particular services, nor is it to devalue the genuine service that is offered. Neither does it question the vocation of Catholic funeral directors and their role in the church's ministry. However, in all this, it is important for the church to fulfill the ministry that is its responsibility and privilege to exercise — a ministry that no director or funeral home can replace. It is in the context of the ecclesial community that Christians are made, married, reconciled, healed and gather Sunday after Sunday. It is within that same ecclesial context that the church's ministry of consolation and prayer takes place. The funeral home is not an ecclesial environment.

At the funeral of a Christian, part of the work of the community of believers is to proclaim its beliefs and values. The Christian community's response in the face of death is rooted in the paschal mystery. This is not the work of funeral directors. While they undertake the work of preparation and transfer of the body, and that work is embraced by the community of faith, the OCF reminds pastors and other ministers that they are "to ensure that undertakers appreciate the values and beliefs of the Christian community" (OCF, 20). This requires communication with funeral directors in forums of mutual respect for the professional services of the funeral director and the ministry of the church. Where efforts toward this kind of communication have taken place, the result is usually a healthy and welcome collaboration.

The service offered by the funeral industry occurs at the end of life and serves very practical purposes. Through the ministry of the community of faith, the church strongly asserts that while death is indeed an ending, its concern is with life, a life that, paradoxically, while ended, is reborn beyond the grave. This belief calls into question much of the mortuary practice that attempts to mask the ending of life: ensuring that the deceased looks as life-like as possible, reclining on a satin-lined inner-spring bed of comfort. The purpose of viewing the body of the deceased is surely not to compare one mortician's art with another's, nor to assess the skill involved in ensuring that the deceased looks as far as possible not dead, but sleeping. Excessively cosmetic embalming is very different from a practice that simply preserves the body for the duration of the rites. Such embalming is the same sort of practice as those that discourage people from completing their care of the deceased in honest rites of committal, or that protect mourners from the harshness and finality of death with discreet graveside cover-up. The church's ministry at the time of death can have no hand in avoidance. In confrontation with death, in a faith-filled ecclesial context, the believing community can afford to be bold, fearless and true, facing things as they are. In the midst of loss and intense pain, Christians can indeed grieve and lament their loss, and at the same time taunt death with the question: O death, where is your victory now?

In Death There Are No Distinctions

It is not uncommon to hear priests and pastoral ministers express a certain frustration that in many funeral situations they are dealing with the "unchurched," as if to wish for a separate formula for such circumstances. Certainly, a funeral is a unique gathering and its assembly is usually far from homogeneous in matters of faith, religious conviction, values and practice. It is unfortunate that the term "unchurched" has crept into our vocabulary as a designation for those who for a variety of reasons do not have regular association with the institutional church. The OCF does not make distinctions among churchgoing believers and non-churchgoing believers, or believers who, for one reason or another, may be estranged from the church. In fact, in placing the pall on the coffin of the deceased when it is received at the church, the community of faith makes a loud statement that "all are equal in the sight of God" (OCF, 38. See James 2:1 – 9). This is perhaps the first shift that pastoral leaders need to make when they are tempted to speak of the "unchurched." For the OCF, while offering a particular way and language, is not a ritual way that depends on the degree of association with church. Rather, it is a way for all who have been baptized into Christ. Baptism earns a person's right to the church's prayer at the time of death.

With that in mind, it cannot be denied that the unique mix of the funeral gathering often presents a significant pastoral challenge. It may be difficult for presiders to find language that will be credible and convincing for all present and at the same time holds to the hope that Christians proclaim in the face of death. Whatever the mix of the assembly, that hope, deriving from faith in the paschal mystery, must have an assured place. Unfortunately, there are times when ministers may be tempted to do as little as possible when they know that there has been little active involvement with the institutional church on the part of the deceased or those who have gathered. Such situations instead demand attitudes that are non-judgmental, and that pastoral ministers be wary of making assumptions about depth of faith that might dictate what is considered to be appropriate.

A guiding principle for all circumstances of worship is ritual honesty and integrity. This in no way suggests that the concern of ritual honesty is with slavish rubrical adherence to a ritual book. Rather, the concern is to ensure that everything said and done in the ritual environment is truthful about the situation, about the intent of the ritual, and about the faith that is proclaimed. It is important that the words put into people's ears or on their lips are known to be true, and words to which they can give assent. If a person has been separated from the church, then there is ritual dishonesty in declaring in a prayer of intercession that the deceased "was nourished at the table of the Savior." This is simply not true. At the funeral of a Christian, ritual honesty is compromised if, for whatever reason, the word of God that proclaims a confident hope in the defeat of death does not take its rightful place. There are circumstances when readings with a heavy theological tone and couched in theological language, although not dishonest, are just out of place. In gatherings that are very mixed, it is better to choose scriptural readings with accessible images and metaphors. Ritual honesty is certainly a question in choosing and adapting prayers, and particularly in the words spoken at the homily. Dishonesty when speaking in memory of the deceased is easily recognized, and is at all times unacceptable.

> *Angela, nineteen years old, had committed suicide and her parents pleaded with the pastoral minister that the word "suicide" not be mentioned at the funeral. It would be too shameful. Eventually, however, they agreed that the cause of Angela's death could be*

named. Two weeks after the funeral, the priest received a letter from Angela's mother. She wrote that the decision to be honest at the funeral was the best thing that could have happened. Because Angela's suicide had been named in public, they did not have to live with the burden of secrecy.

The pastoral challenge of participation is also a difficult one for funeral assemblies in which there are varying degrees of familiarity with the rituals of the church. The church cannot place its expectations of "full, conscious, and active participation" (*Constitution on the Sacred Liturgy,* 14) on people for whom this particular way of celebrating death is a foreign experience. The bare fact that people have assembled is a participative act. At the same time, there is no denying that voices raised in communal song and prayer carry a power to console and uplift. It is for this reason that a parish needs to have some old favorites in its funeral music repertoire. To assist participation and comfort an order of service that to many may be quite unfamiliar, well-prepared booklets or service sheets are invaluable, making clear the times to sit, stand or kneel, spoken responses and words of hymns. Some parishes have found it helpful to include in these orders of service a simple explanation of the symbols that are used at the funeral service. Whatever is prepared, it must be remembered that the object is participation, not distraction. Hence the prepared order of service needs to be simple and clear, and also flexible enough to include personal touches such as the name of the deceased and the names of those who minister in various ways.

Care is required in circumstances in which the deceased or the mourners may have had little recent association with the church and its rituals. There are simply no circumstances in which the deceased Christian and the bereaved are to be deprived of the church's prayer. The OCF is careful to ensure that in death there can be no distinctions. No particular cause of death renders a person ineligible for the church's prayer. This is to be remembered in the case of people who have died of HIV/AIDS.

There are, however, certain pastoral concerns that arise in the case of people who die of HIV/AIDS. While not all AIDS deaths are related to homosexuality, the majority of such situations in the Western world do involve the homosexual community, a community well aware of its own pain, victimization and alienation. Many have experienced rejection, isolation and anger, and in this, families and the church have not remained guiltless. At the time of death, such circumstances clearly call for an inclusive and caring environment. They demand the presence, the hospitality and welcome of the church, and ask of pastoral ministers attitudes free of prejudice and judgment at all times.

All this must be evident in the funeral rites. As the church welcomes and acknowledges the principal mourner at any funeral, so too the church must welcome the principal mourner at the funerals of those who die of AIDS. This means acknowledgment of the partner and thus the relationship, acknowledgment of the gay community as well as of the deceased's biological family. As always, honesty is crucial. There may be conflict, among the family, the partner and the family of choice, that is, the devoted friends of the deceased, regarding the mention of AIDS at the funeral. This situation requires pastoral skills and respect, on the part of the minister, for the wishes of the partner. There is great potential for public denial at the funeral of a person who has died of AIDS, but dishonesty and denial only mean more of the pretense which, regrettably, many have experienced in life. Nor is there room for homilists who indulge in tirades condemning ways of life. Unprejudiced and non-judgmental attitudes honor the fact that all are equal in the sight of God.

For people living and dying with AIDS, the body, in its very ravaging, assumes a vital importance. The church assures all who die that it will respect and honor their bodies "since in baptism the body was marked with the seal of the Trinity and became the temple of the Holy Spirit" (OCF, 19). Hence, the reverent honor given to the body is of particular significance at funerals of those who die of AIDS. The importance of gestures of profound reverence — such as bowing, touching the coffin, sprinkling with water, clothing with the pall, circling the coffin with clouds of incense — cannot be overestimated. They speak of a church ever ready to claim the deceased as one of its own, to care reverently for the bodies of those who have died.

People dying of AIDS often prepare their own funerals. There may be requests for particular readings that may not be scriptural, for songs that may not be "religious," for reading of poems and letters, for use of the rainbow flag. Provided that the church's proclamation of hope grounded in the death and resurrection of Jesus is not compromised, pastoral sensitivity to human needs suggests that these might be incorporated into the rituals. The principles guiding their use are the same as for any other funeral. The community of people with AIDS has already contributed richly to rituals surrounding dying and grieving. In their lighting of candles and their piecing together of quilts, for example, they have demonstrated the need to deal with grief in some kind of public way, and to find fitting frameworks in which to express grief, sorrow and love, to weep and pray together. If that can be done within the welcoming and caring environment of a faith community that lovingly cares for its deceased and the bereaved, all will be enriched.

Rituals for Termination of Life Support and for Donation of Organs

Modern medicine has discovered a vast array of new and radical methods aimed at saving and lengthening lives. The debates about euthanasia, assisted suicide, living wills and other choices about dying force us into serious and unprecedented thinking about the meaning and place of death in our lives.

In this new era of being able to prolong life, or delay death, families are often faced with difficult decisions concerning the continuation or withdrawal of aggressive technological methods of life support. There is unavoidable tension around such decision-making, often accompanied by feelings of fear, guilt, ambivalence and sadness. In such times there is little to guide us and little to help us carry the burden of responsibility and emotion. Whereas we have rituals and a body of prayer surrounding natural dying and death that help us to negotiate these difficult moments, this is not the case with withdrawal of systems of life support.

Pastoral workers and chaplains in hospitals face a variety of situations in cases where people are on life support systems or mechanical ventilators. There are cases when the person is alive but unconscious, and death is delayed by means of life support systems; the person is brain dead, that is, actually dead, but the action of a mechanical ventilator provides the visible appearance of life; or the person is brain dead and body functions are being sustained by mechanical means for the ultimate purpose of donating organs or donating the body to science.

No official books provide rites to join ritual and prayer to a family's decision to cease life support, although there are a few resources for such prayer in other places.[16] In joining prayer to these occasions, it is crucial that the pastoral minister be mindful of the emotional intensity of the situation and of the pastoral needs of those present; every case will surely be different. Such prayer must be brief and focused. Inspiration for ritual actions, prayers and other texts could be drawn from our rites for commendation of the dying and prayers for the dead.[17]

A possible order of service for the removal of a life-support system from a person who is alive but unconscious or of a mechanical ventilator from a person who is brain dead could be identical. The difference would be that, in the latter case, when the person is in fact dead, the prayers would acknowledge that death has occurred.

Introductory Rite

This could begin with an invitation to prayer and an introduction that acknowledges and gives thanks for the life now ending. The minister might then call on God, the author of life and death, for strength and comfort. Words expressing the desire to commend the dying to God also belong here.

Liturgy of the Word

This could include a short and appropriate scripture reading or psalm (Psalm 22 is very apt), and a brief prayer of intercession to be followed by the Our Father. The liturgy of the word might conclude with the Canticle of Simeon (Luke 2:29 – 32): "Now let your servant die in peace . . ." and be followed by words such as "Let us now unbind N. and let her/him go free, that she/he might enter eternal life and joy."

Commendation and Farewell

Those present might make a final gesture of farewell. The act of removal of the life support system or ventilator would then take place. A prayer of commendation might accompany or follow the act.

Concluding Rite

The rite could conclude with a prayer for the dying or the deceased, a prayer for the family and friends, and a blessing.

This order of service could be adapted for cases of donation of organs or of the body to science. It is important to recognize that even though the life support system provides the appearance of life, the person is in fact dead, and honesty demands that this be named. In such situations it is important that a hospital representative be present for the prayer. The act, in this case, is not the removal of systems but the handing over of the body to the care of the hospital authorities. This would occur after the liturgy of the word. This act could consist of a memorial of baptism, if this seems appropriate, the act of entrusting the body to the hospital authorities, and the acceptance of the body by the hospital representative.

Family and friends:
We entrust the body of N. to your care.
Lord, as we take leave of N.,
give our hearts comfort
in the firm hope that he/she will live in your peace.

Hospital representative:
On behalf of those who will benefit by this gift,
we take the body of N. into our care.

This act would then be followed by the commendation and farewell and the concluding rite.

The need for keen pastoral sensitivity on these occasions cannot be overstated. It is important that ministers be flexible in their use of any form of prayer and that they be attentive at all times to the pastoral needs of those concerned and to the circumstances of each situation. Prayer and faith brought to these painful and intense occasions offer to the family an opportunity to experience some degree of completion and ownership of an action which is intensely difficult, to know some peace of mind as a result of their decision, and to affirm their belief that ultimately it is God who is the author of life and death.

Conclusion

Not long ago I heard a radio interview with a historian. The moderator asked her: "How would you assess the effects of the 18th-century Industrial Revolution?" After some moments of pondering, the historian answered, "It's a bit too early to tell!" At this early stage of implementation of the *Order of Christian Funerals,* we might be tempted to make a similar assessment of its success. After all, it is only ten years since its publication, and we are only some thirty years past Vatican II.

The response of one parish that takes seriously ministry at the time of death and has taken up the challenge of the OCF is "It's a winner." The OCF with its rich ritual process comes at a time when we have become more and more aware of Western society's allegedly death-denying ways, of the de-ritualizing of secular society, of the paucity of collective cultural responses to the reality of death. One contemporary writer, commenting on the tendency toward a minimalist response to death, notes:

> In our secular society the ceremonies that traditionally surrounded death have been gradually eliminated, leaving little to replace them. For most of us there will be no last rites, no final anointing, no confession, no candles, no vigils, no holy oil, no prayers, no masses, no requiems, no wakes, little or no

public grieving, and nowadays sometimes not even flowers for the grave. . . . We conduct quick, in-out funerals, and believe twenty-minute services . . . "quite long" . . . When I look for reasons I can find only one. *Because it is too difficult.* The pain just makes it *too* hard.[1]

Yet while it might not be difficult to concur with this assessment, one journalist recorded at the time of the death of Diana, Princess of Wales, that "one of the most striking features . . . [was] the extraordinarily high profile of religion in it all. . . . Without quite realizing what it was doing, or why, a post-Christian, post-Protestant nation found itself praying for the dead."[2] And this tragic death has not been the only occasion when our generation has witnessed, on the world stage, an extraordinarily high profile of behavior in the face of death that was highly ritualized, if not overtly religious. Maybe we are not so death-denying, so bereft of ritual instincts after all.

While our society might well be accused of a minimalist response to death, perhaps "in the hope of minimizing the pain of death,"[3] perhaps there is at this time very fertile soil in which the pastoral and ritual vision of the OCF might take firm root. But the publication of a new book (or a now ten-year-old book) will not of itself make this happen. There is work to be done if the deceased of our communities and those who mourn their death are to be surrounded by liturgical assemblies of consolation and prayer. There is work to be done if, in a culture that fears death as the annihilating enemy, the message of Christian hope and death-as-friend is to be proclaimed. There is work to be done if our ritual care at the time of death is to do its work of proclaiming the transforming power of the death and resurrection of Jesus, a mystery of faith which offers promise and hope in the midst of death and the pain of loss.

This book has not attempted to answer all questions concerning our use of the OCF. In fact, the increased use of its rites seems to result in yet more questions. It might be too early to evaluate its overall success, but I am sure that communities that have taken up the challenge of this work of ritual and pastoral care have already experienced its rich potential — for the deceased, for those who mourn and for themselves. In its counter-cultural stance of calling into question a minimalist response to death; in its vision of a community that recognizes its baptismal responsibility for care and consolation at the time of death; in its ensemble of rites through which the deceased and those who mourn are surrounded by an assembly of prayer from a person's last days through burial and beyond; in its invitation to the bereaved to bring their grief to the safe environment of a community of faith; in its confident proclamation that the death of a Christian is embraced by the transforming death of Jesus; in its remarkable potential to transform communities into energetic communities of care — the *Order of Christian Funerals* is indeed a most powerful way to face death together.

Introduction

1. Margaret Hebblethewaite, "The princess at peace," *The Tablet,* 13 September 1997, 1155.

2. Cardinal Basil Hume, "Through death to new life," *The Tablet,* 13 September 1997, 1154.

3. *Order of Christian Funerals.* Prepared by the International Commission on English in the Liturgy, a Joint Commission of Catholic Bishops' Conferences. Approved by the Sacred Congregation for Divine Worship, 1989.

4. The first post–Vatican II revision of the rite for funerals resulted in the ritual book entitled *The Rite of Funerals* (1969). A revision of this first-generation ritual book was initiated by ICEL in 1980. The result of that revision is the *Order of Christian Funerals.* In this sense it can be called a second-generation ritual book.

Chapter 1

1. C. S. Lewis, *A Grief Observed* (New York: Bantam, 1963), 35.

2. Kevin Hart, "Haranguing Death," in *New and Selected Poems* (Sydney: HarperCollins, 1995).

Chapter 2

1. The Oklahoma City bombing and the massacres at Dunblane in Scotland and Port Arthur in Australia are examples of such tragedies.

2. Richard Rutherford, *The Order of Christian Funerals: Invitation to Pastoral Care,* American Essays in Liturgy Series, ed. Edward Foley (Collegeville, MN: The Liturgical Press, 1990), 14.

3. Gerald Arbuckle, *Change, Grief and Renewal in the Church: A Spirituality for a New Era* (Westminster, MD: Christian Classics, 1991), 28.

Chapter 3

1. *Order of Christian Funerals,* 111. Approved by the Irish Bishops' Conference for use in the dioceses of Ireland.

2. Liturgy Training Publications' small prayerbook series has titles that contain many of these domestic prayers from the ritual books. For the OCF's prayers after death, see *Prayers with the Dying,* pages 50–61. For the OCF's gathering in the presence of the body, see *Prayers of Those Who Mourn,* pages 1–8. Also in that book is the rite of transfer of the body, but here titled "Prayers before Taking the Body to Church," (pages 18–22). The OCF's rite of gathering in the presence of the body and transfer of the body are also printed on participation cards by LTP, under the title *Funeral Home Prayer Cards.* Prayers from the *Pastoral Care of the Sick* to use at the bedside of one dying are also excerpted in *Prayers with the*

Dying, and the rites of penance, communion and anointing of the sick are all found in *Rites of the Sick.*

3. See, for example, *Life is Changed, Not Ended: A Workbook for Preparing a Catholic Funeral,* ed. Tom Elich (Brisbane: Liturgical Commission, 1996). For the ritual order on participation cards to be used by the assembly, see Liturgy Training Publications' *Vigil for the Deceased: Participation Cards.*

4. If the vigil is celebrated at the church, it incorporates a formal reception of the body as part of the service. This will be discussed in the following chapter.

5. The Office for the Dead is discussed separately on pages 55–58.

6. Had there been a wake chapel in this church, the vigil would have taken place there.

7. Mary Wickham, RSM, "Deaf One," *In the Water Was the Fire* (Melbourne: Spectrum Publications, 1995).

8. See the collection of funeral music *In the Peace of Christ.* Christopher Willcock (Melbourne: CollinsDove, 1993).

9. The particular setting was John Bell's "Let Your Restless Heart Be Still" from *The Last Journey: Songs for the Time of Grieving* (Chicago: GIA, 1997).

10. A number of fine settings of the Nunc Dimittis exist. The one sung on this occasion was from Christopher Willcock, *In the Peace of Christ* (Melbourne: CollinsDove, 1993).

11. See *General Instruction of the Liturgy of the Hours,* 38.

Chapter 4

1. The point made in this discussion raises the wider question of the suitability of many of our places of worship, not only for our funeral rites but for all the reformed rites of the church. We have a new liturgy which often cannot do its work because of the inflexibility of the spaces in which we pray them.

2. This text is not included in the OCF for use in Australia or in the United States, although it was proposed in an earlier draft. It seems unfortunate that a text accompanies the sprinkling with water, but not for the less familiar action — at least in Australia — of placing the pall.

3. This point will be taken up in more detail in the final section of this book.

4. Kenneth R. Mitchell and Herbert Anderson, *All Our Losses, All Our Griefs* (Philadelphia: Westminster Press, 1983), 159.

5. The OCF provides a rite of committal with final commendation for use when no funeral liturgy has preceded the committal rite. See OCF, 205, 224–233.

6. Joy Gardner-Gordon, "Learning to Use the Sound That Heals," *Natural Health* (May/June 1994): 46.

7. Robin Green, *Intimate Mystery: Our Need to Worship* (Cambridge, MA: Cowley Publications, 1988), 13.

Chapter 5

1. John Dear, "'Sleep well,' friends tell Henri Nouwen," *National Catholic Reporter* (October 11, 1996): 13.

2. Kerry Cue, *Australia Unbuttoned* (Ringwood, Victoria: Penguin Books Australia, 1996), 159.

3. See Canon 1176.3; the 1969 *Ordo Exsequiarum*, 15; OCF, 19.

4. Robert Hovda, "Amen Corner," *Worship* 59:3 (May, 1985): 225.

5. Committee on the Liturgy, National Conference of Catholic Bishops, *Reflections on the Body, Cremation, and Catholic Funeral Rites* (Washington: United States Catholic Conference, 1997), 9.

6. Ibid., 10.

7. The Australian bishops have published an outline order of service. The Irish bishops have included in an appendix a complete order of service for cremation. The OCF for use in Canada provides detailed pastoral notes for purposes of cremation. The Bishops' Conference of England and Wales provides seven fully laid out services for a variety of circumstances of committal, including three for cremation and one for the burial of ashes. These committal rites are available in a separate ritual book. It is useful for pastoral ministers to have access to these other editions of the OCF.

8. For ease of use, it would be simple for pastoral ministers to assemble orders of service for this rite similar to that previously mentioned.

9. Note that that disposal of the body as soon as possible after death is a treasured value in other faith traditions, and is constitutive of reverent care of the body of the deceased. This discussion is not intended to criticize practices of other faiths. Rather, it seeks to address the issue within the context of Catholic beliefs and values.

10. The Appendix is available from Liturgy Training Publications in pamphlet form, and will be included in new printings of the OCF.

11. See Appendix IV, OCF [Canada].

12. See OCF [England and Wales], 239.

13. *Reflections on the Body, Cremation and Catholic Funeral Rites,* 11.

Chapter 6

1. James McAuley, "Pietà," in *Anthology of Australian Religious Poetry,* ed. Les A. Murray (Melbourne: CollinsDove, 1986). Reprinted by permission of HarperCollins Publishers.

Chapter 7

1. Paul Janowiak, SJ. "The Assembly and the Paschal Mystery." *Liturgy 90* (July 1997): 10.

2. Acknowledgment is made of the insights and writings of Deirdre Browne, IBVM, a widely respected musician of the church of Australia.

3. Huub Oosterhuis, "The Tent of Meeting," in *Prayers, Poems and Songs* (New York, Herder and Herder, 1970). Quoted in *Prayers of Those Who Make Music* (Chicago: Liturgy Training Publications, 1981), 42.

4. See the music of John Bell, *The Last Journey* (Chicago: GIA, 1996); Christopher Willcock, *In the Peace of Christ* (Melbourne: CollinsDove, 1993). Also see David Haas, *Blessed Are Those Who Mourn* (Chicago: GIA, 1997).

5. See *RitualSong, Worship, Gather,* all from GIA; *Gather Australia,* NLMC/GIA.

6. Michael Joncas, arr., *Music for Christian Funerals: Six Hymns with Descants* (Schiller Park, IL: World Library Publications, 1990).

7. National Association of Pastoral Musicians, *The Milwaukee Symposia for Church Musicians* (Chicago: Liturgy Training Publications, 1992), 74.

8. U.S. Bishops' Committee on the Liturgy, *Liturgical Music Today,* 60.

9. Paul Duffy, *Word of Life in Media and Gospel* (Sydney: St. Paul Publications, 1991), 15.

10. Ibid.

11. *The Milwaukee Symposia for Church Composers,* 78.

12. See, for example, Liturgy Training Publications, *Prayers of Those Who Mourn,* 44 – 46.

13. Gabrielle Carey, "A Death-Denying Circus," in *The Penguin Book of Death,* Gabrielle Carey and Rosemary Sorensen, eds. (Ringwood, Victoria: Penguin Books Australia, 1997), 113.

14. See *Prayers of Those Who Mourn,* 45 – 48.

15. Carey, *op. cit.,* 113.

16. Two collections of simple prayer services designed for such situations are: Shannon, Thomas A. and Charles N. Faso, *Let Them Go Free* (Kansas City: Sheed and Ward, 1987) and O'Loughlin, Francis and Margaret Smith, *Go Forth, Faithful Christian* (Melbourne: Diocesan Liturgical Centre, 1991).

17. See *Pastoral Care of the Sick: Rites of Anointing and Viaticum.*

Conclusion

1. Carey, *op. cit.,* 115 f.

2. Eamon Duffy, "Let us pray," *The Tablet* (6 September 1997): 1117.

3. Carey, *op. cit.,* 116.